Vagabond Mandala Om
by Kathryn Colvig

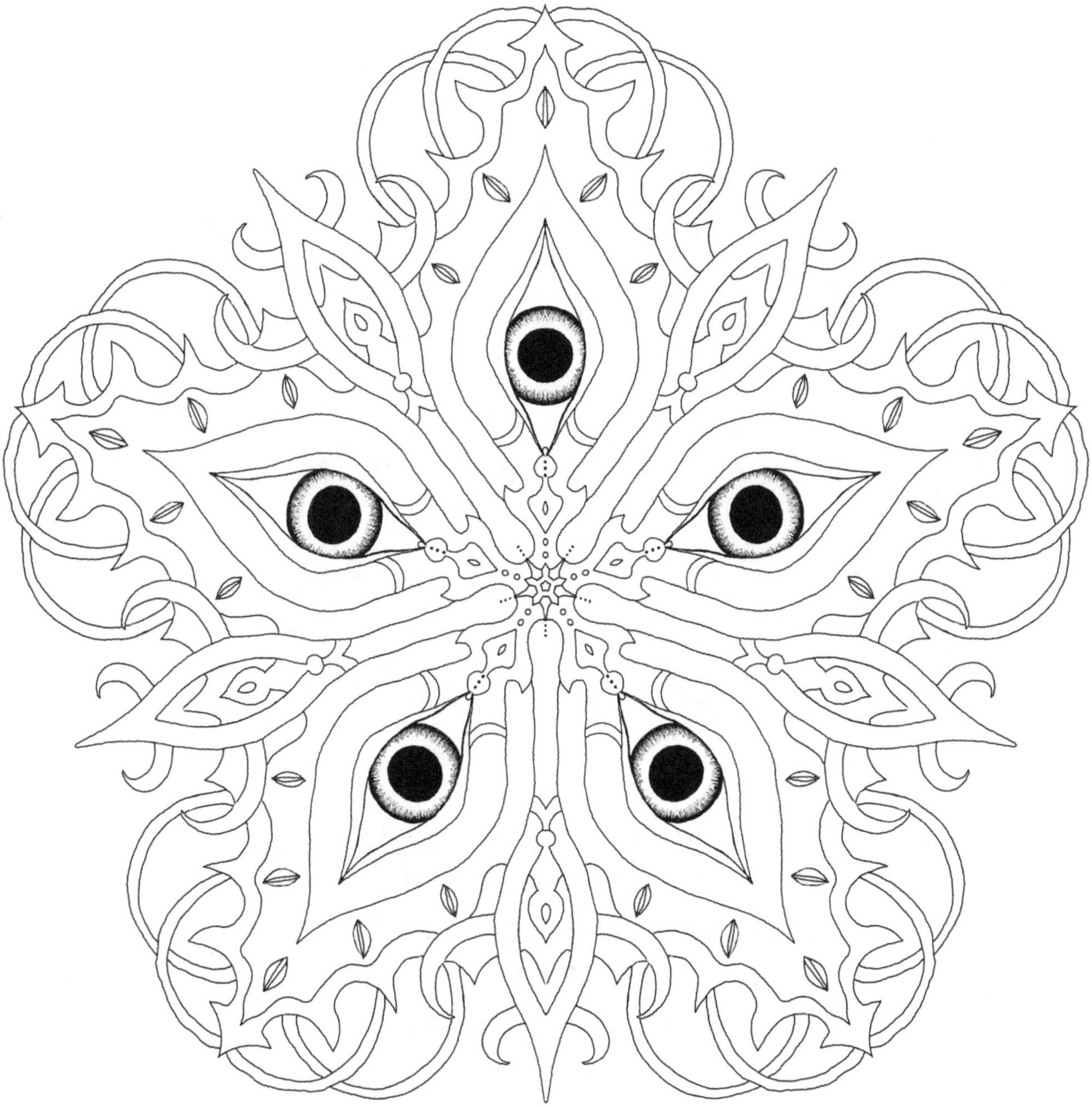

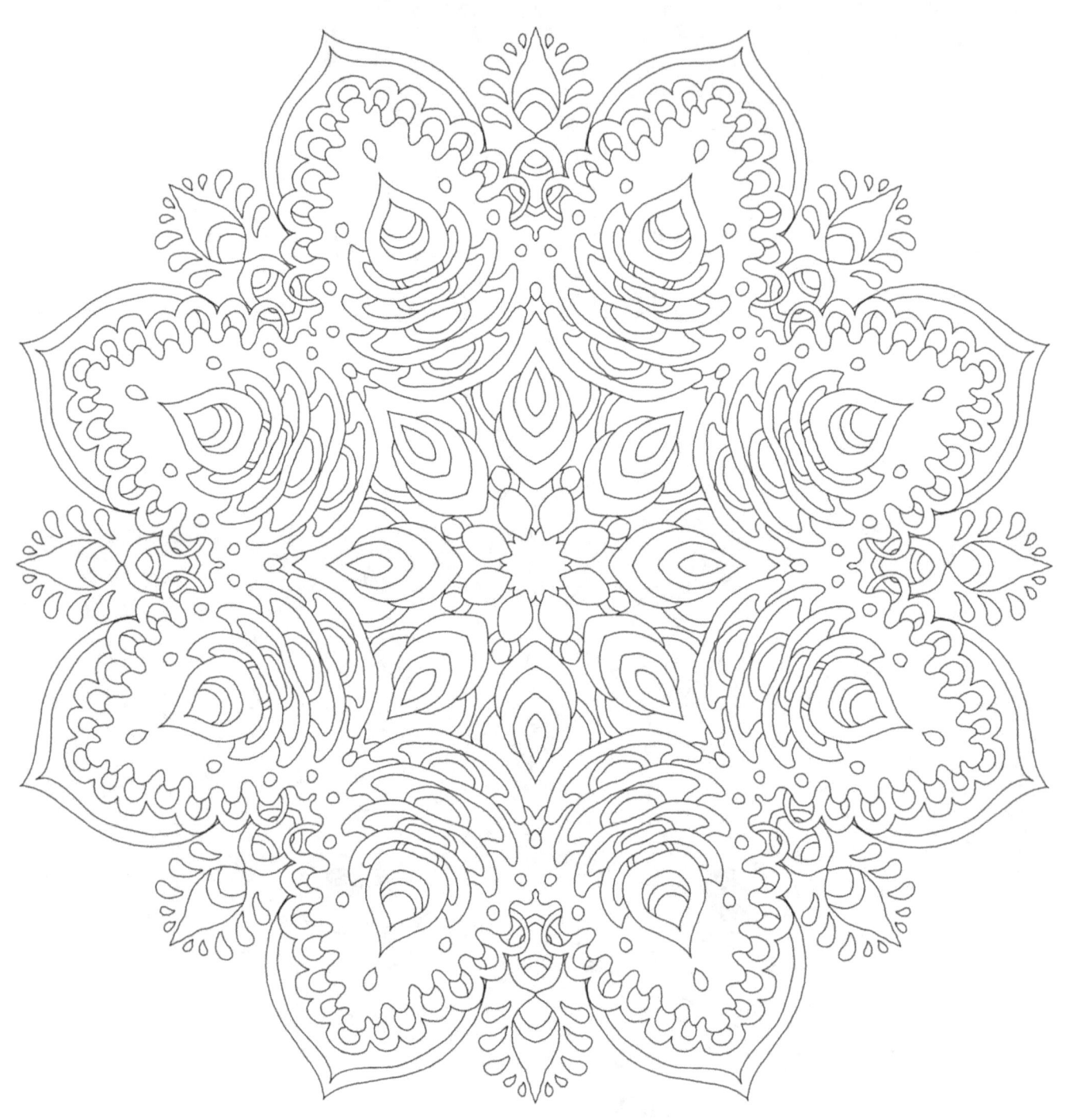

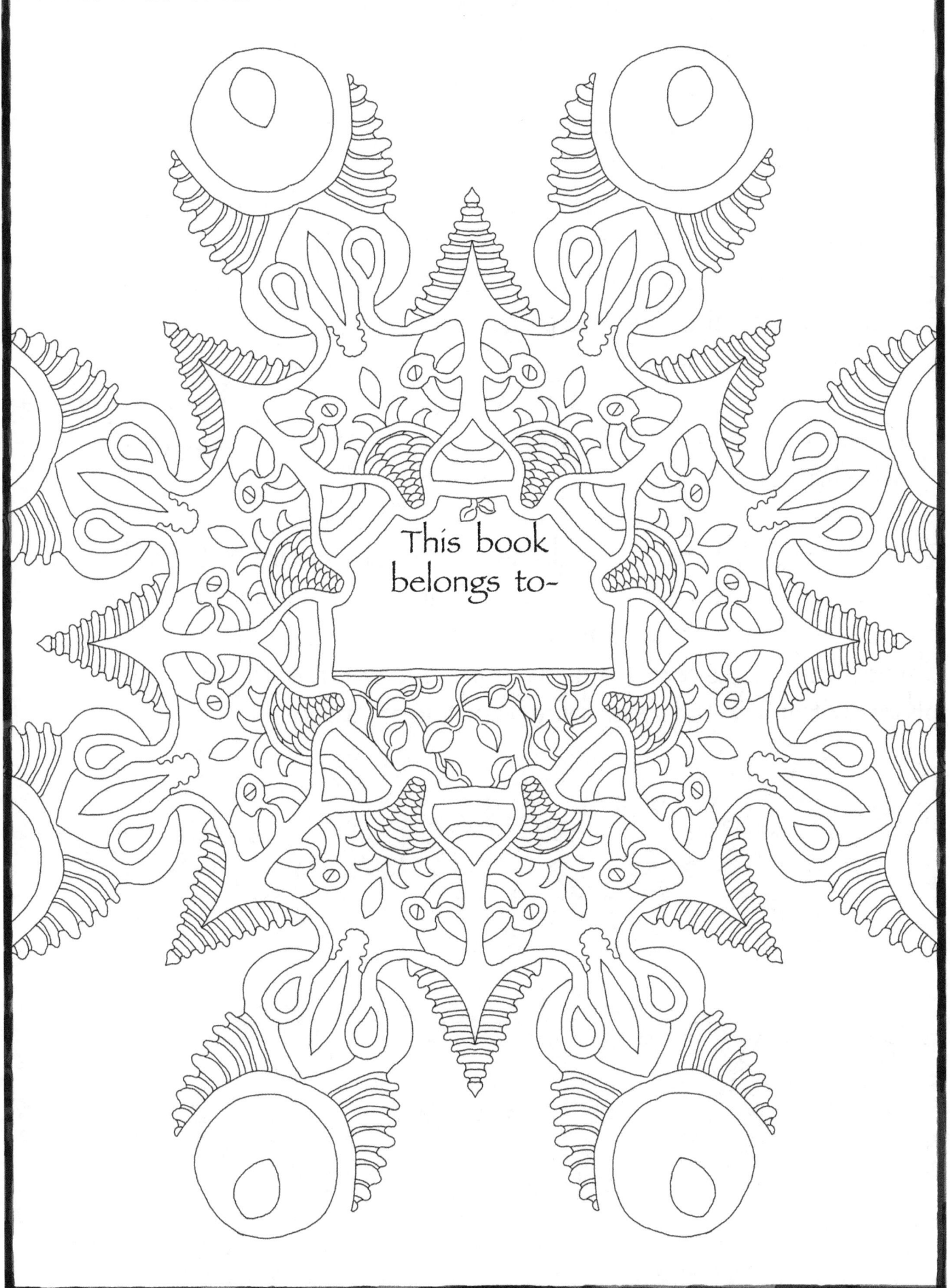

This book
belongs to-

A note from Kathryn~

I have always been fascinated by the mystical designs and patterns of Moroccan and Indian architecture and design. The mosaics, paintings, fabric designs, and carved stone buildings are so beautiful and intricate.

I created Vagabond Mandala Om to honor the beauty and the artists that have inspired me. I have drawn simple, easy mandalas as well as complex ones that really slow you down and focus your intention on the page.

They all help you relax and get out of your head. Coloring has been proven to have the same effect on your brain as meditation. How cool is that? We can all use a little less mind chatter in our daily lives.

There are 25 different Mandalas, and each is printed twice for you to re-create newly with a different palette of color. They are all single sided for use with most media. I do recommend that you place a backing sheet behind your page when using markers or other wet media that may bleed through. Enjoy!

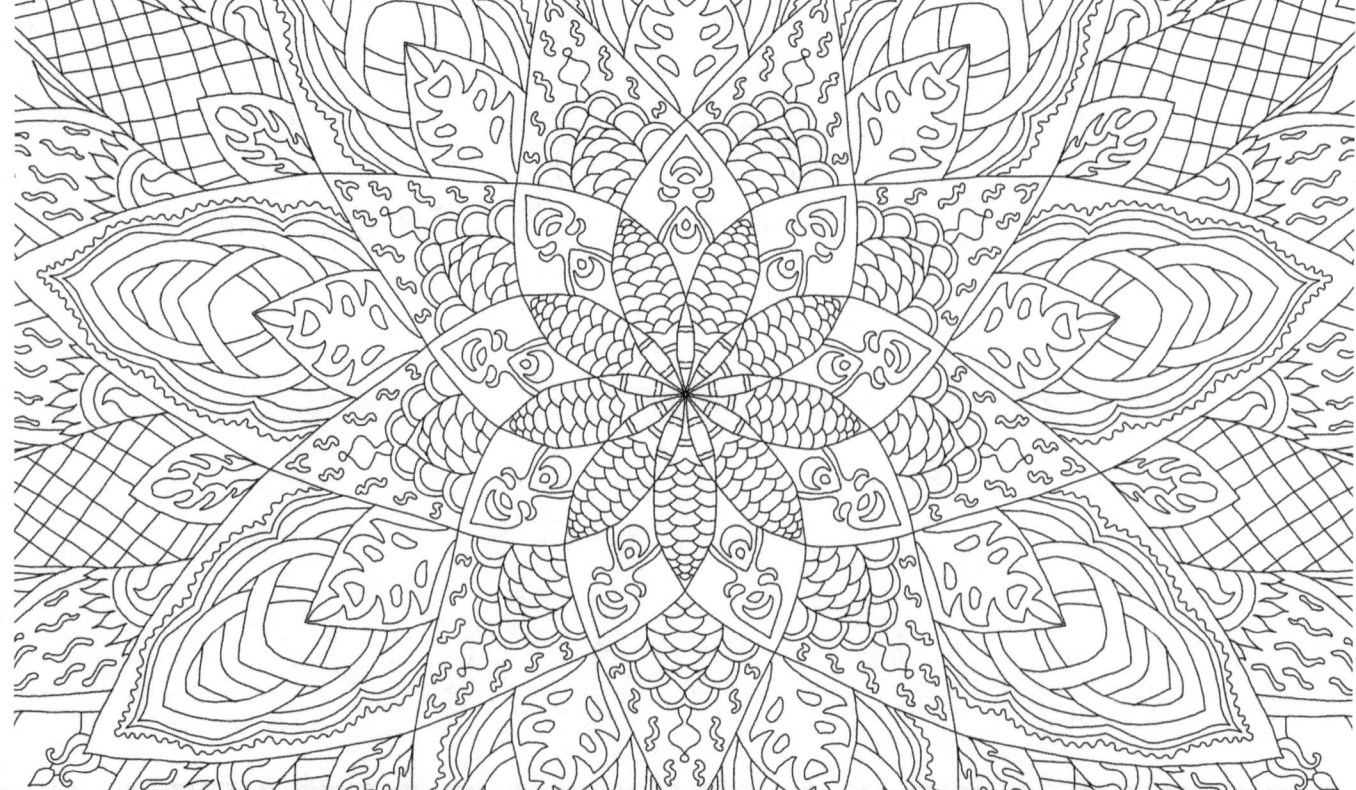

Table of Contents:

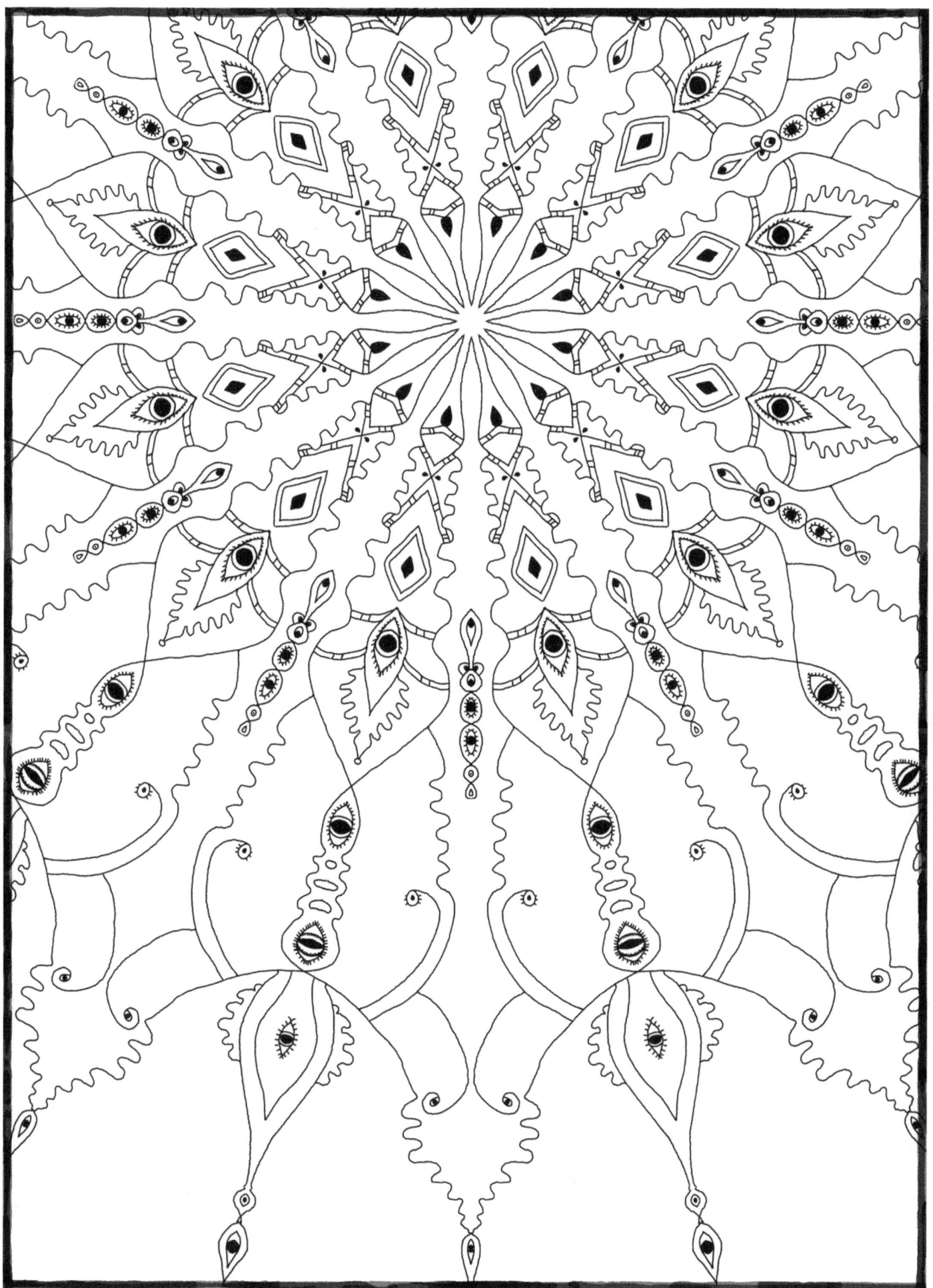

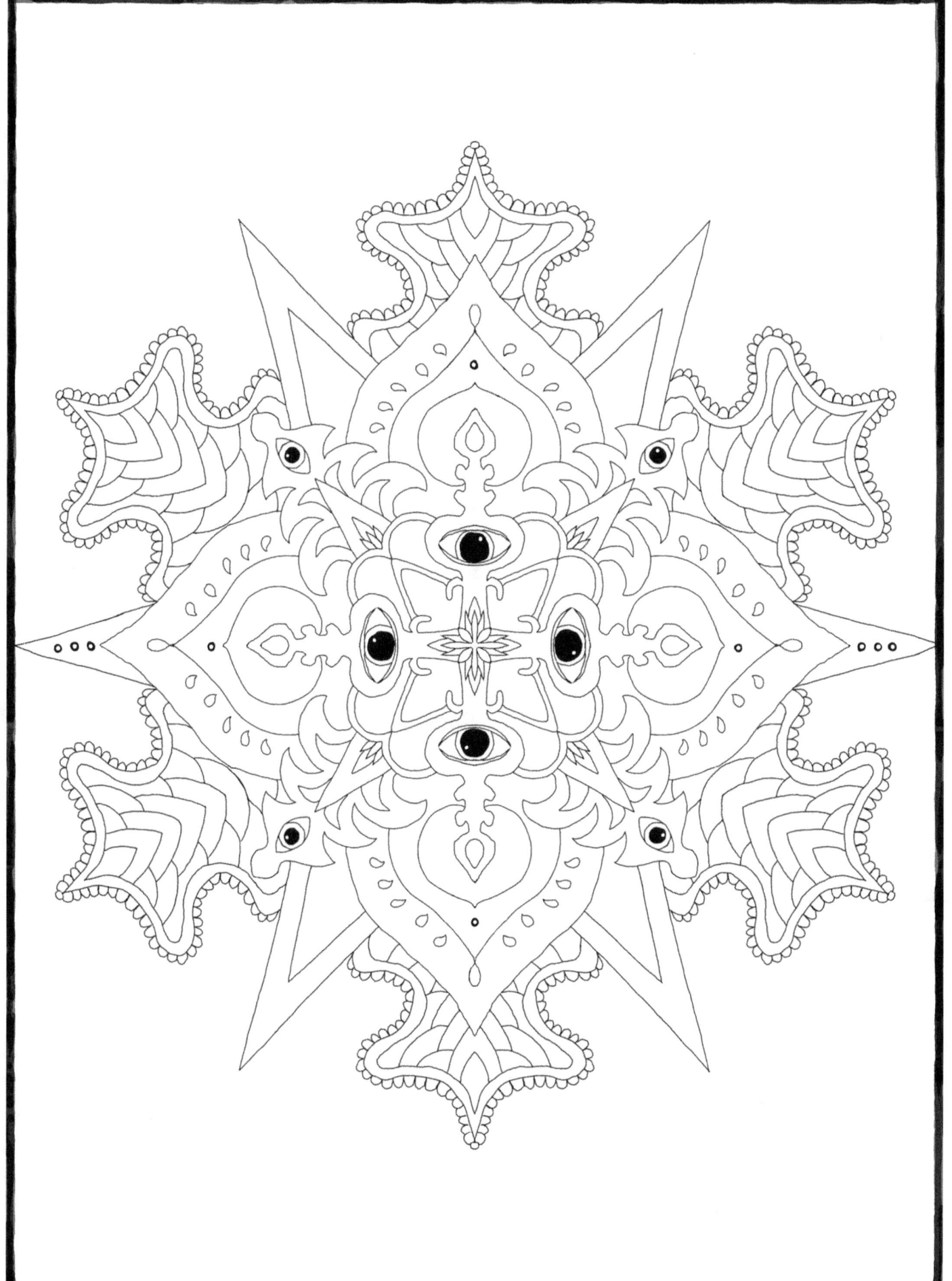

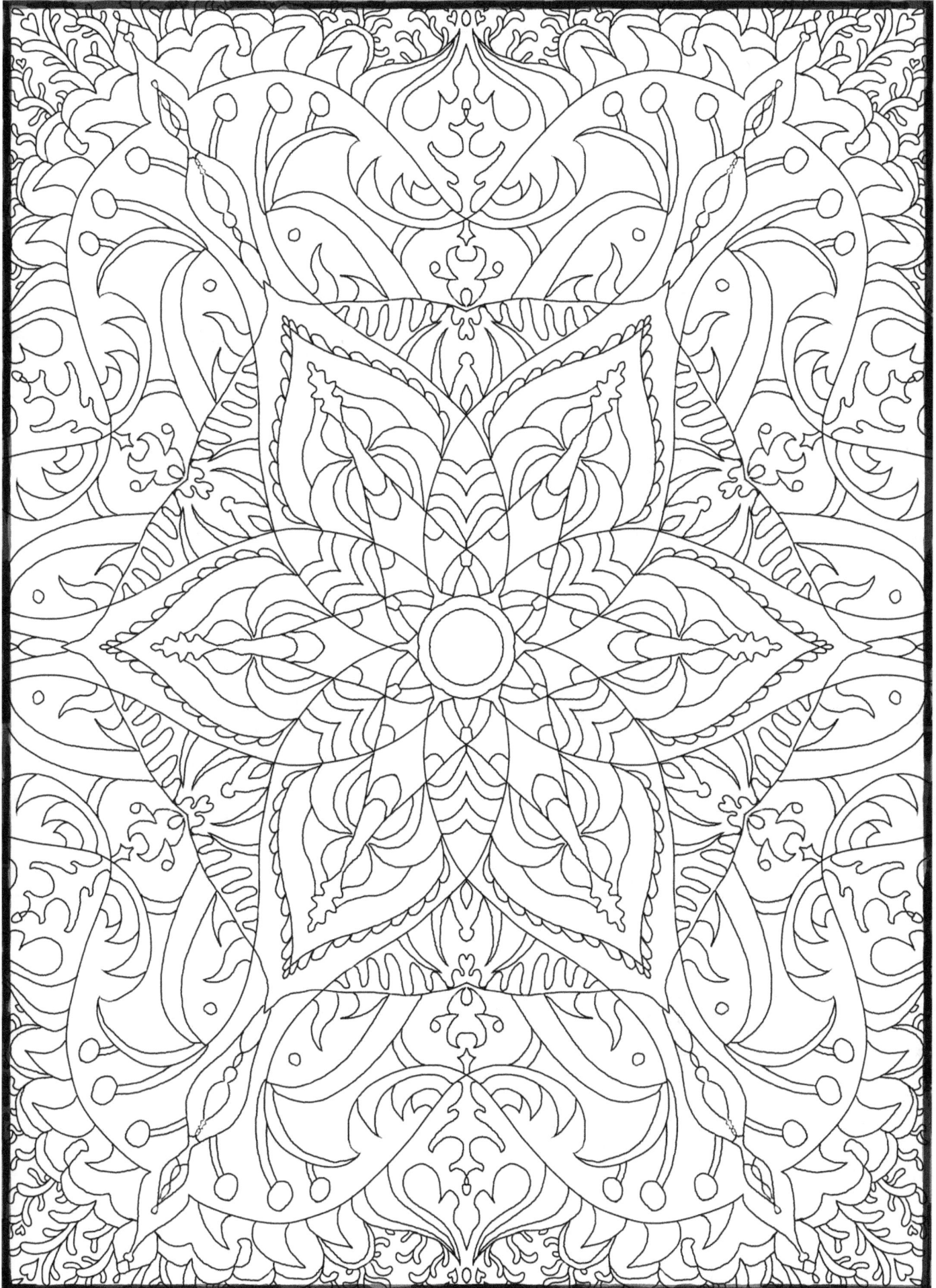

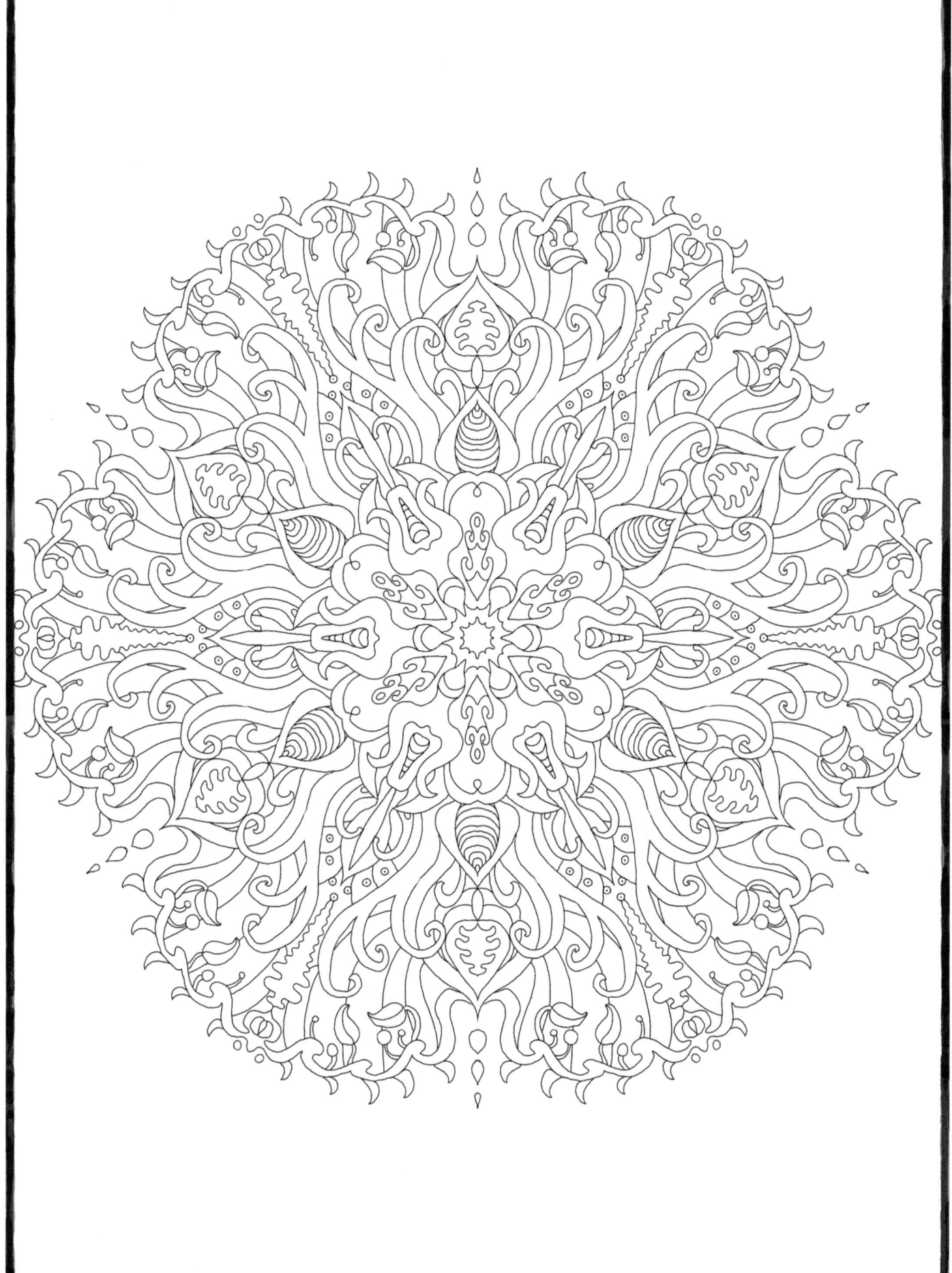

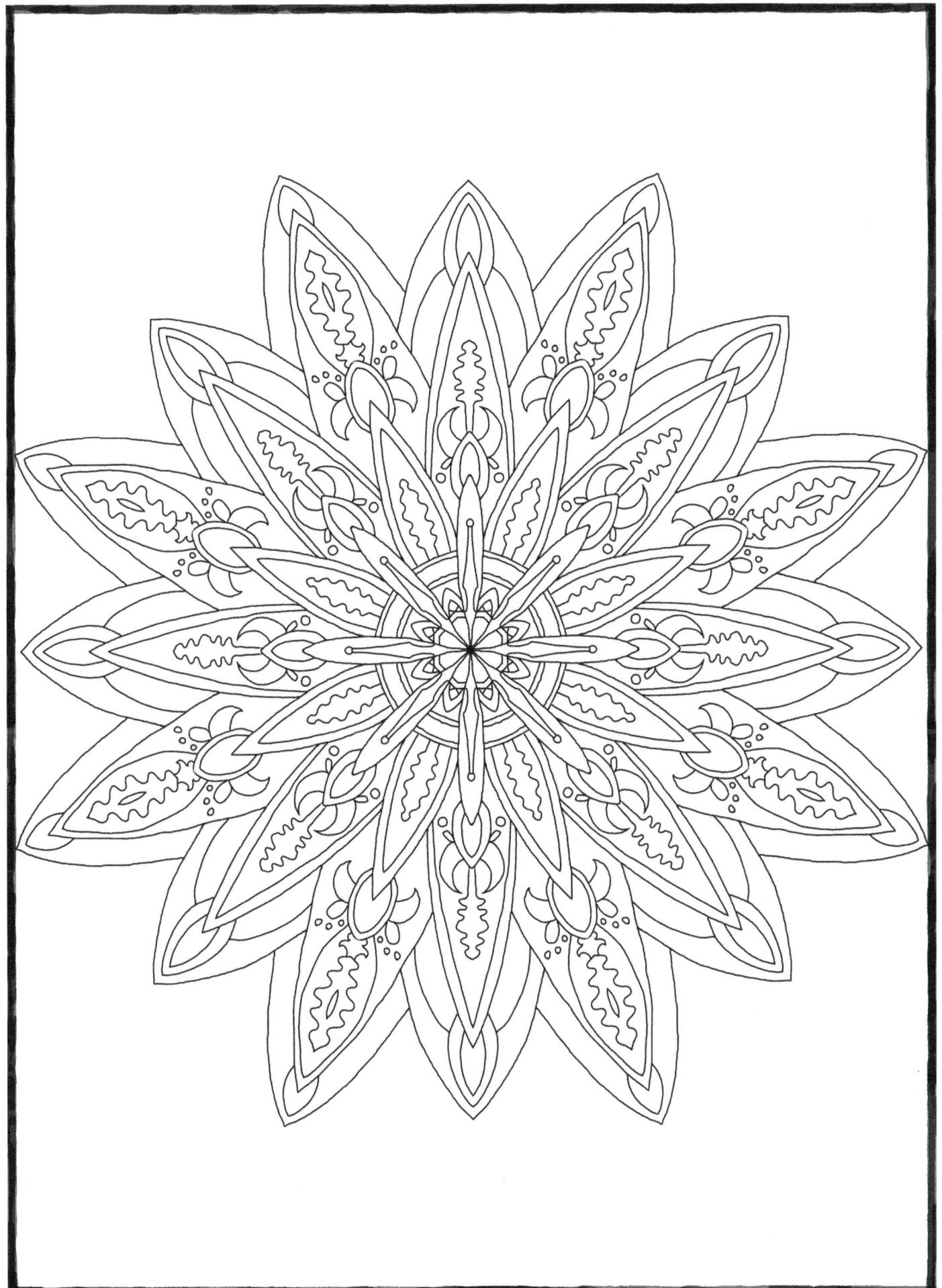

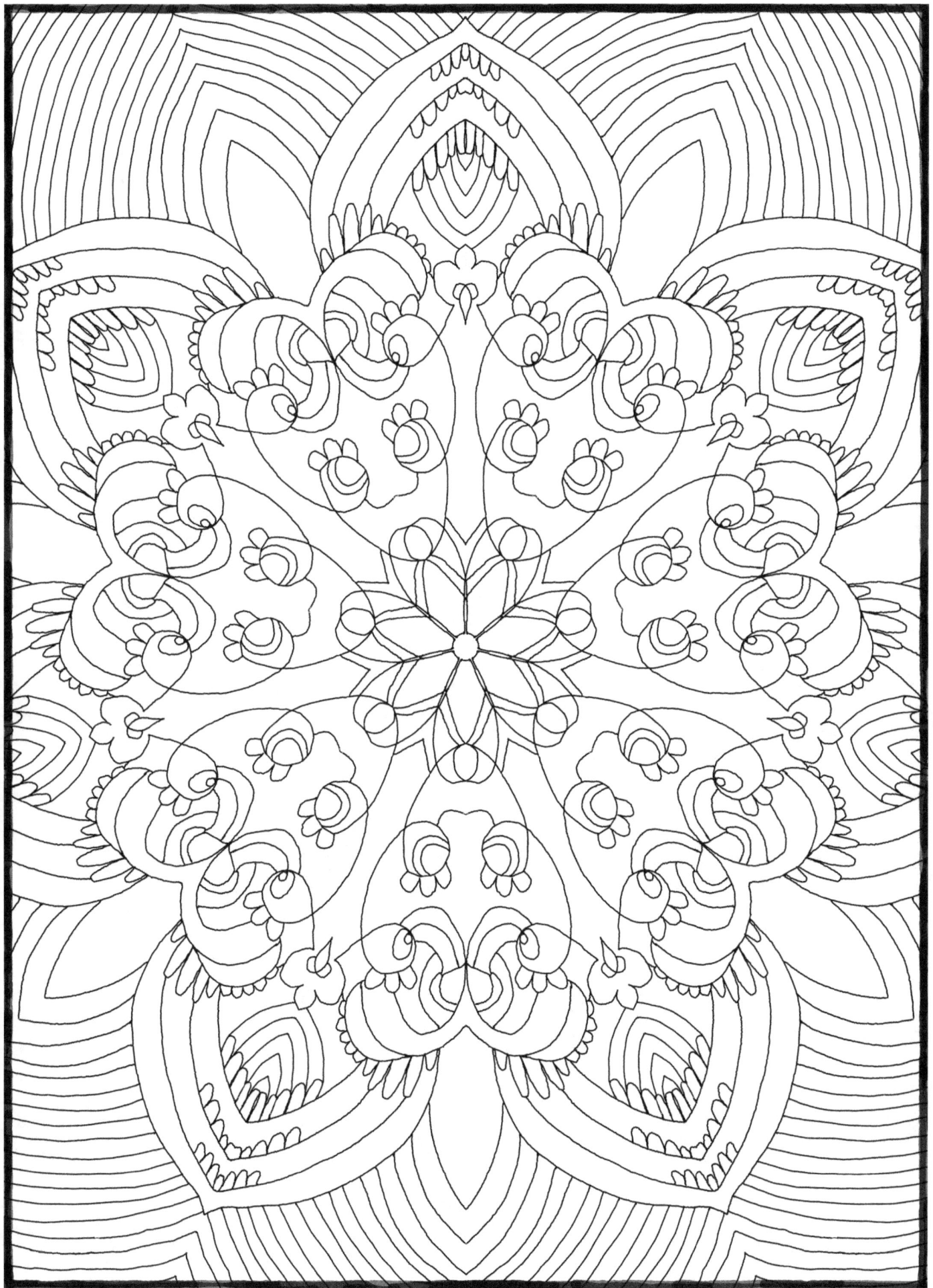

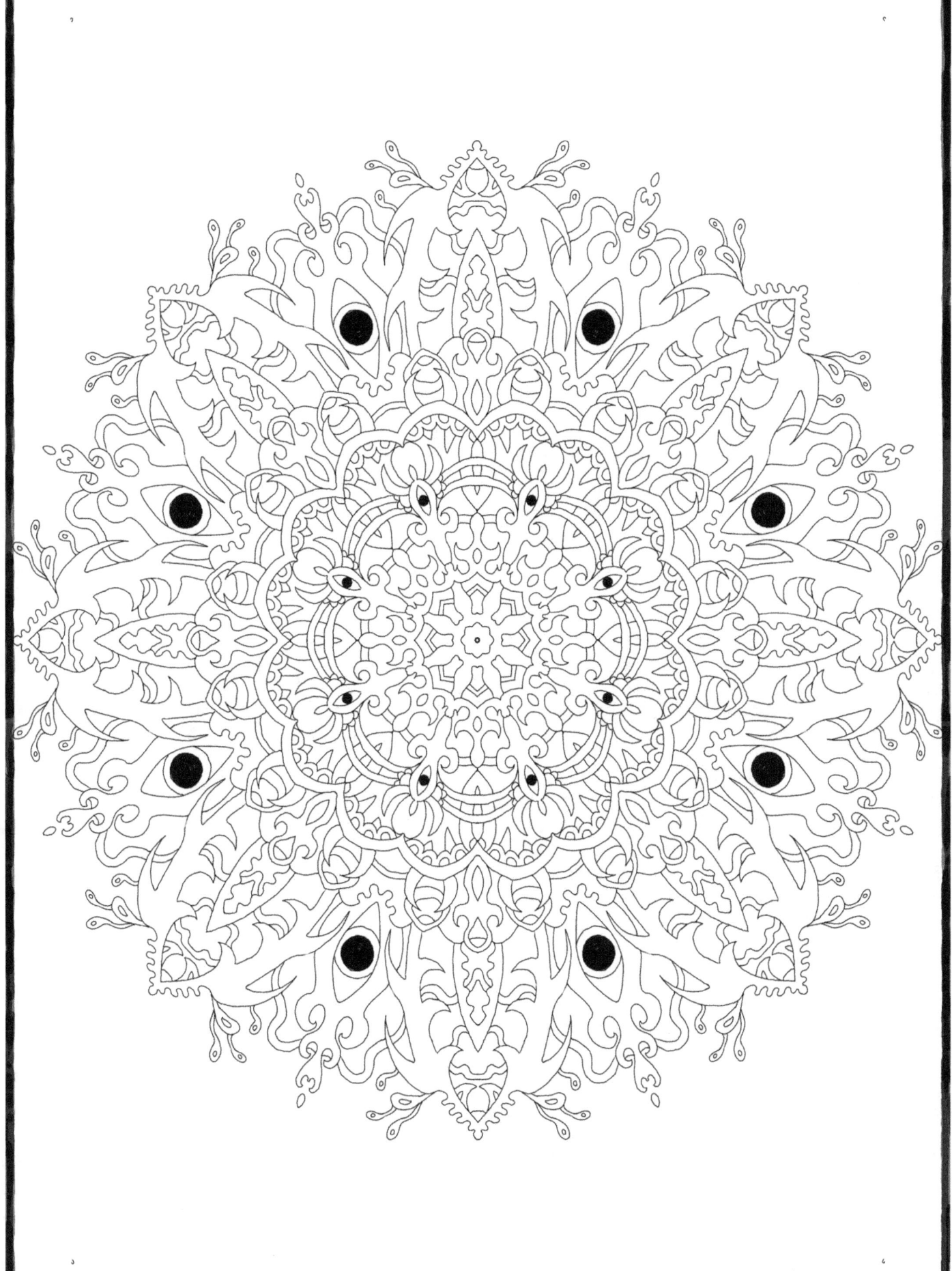

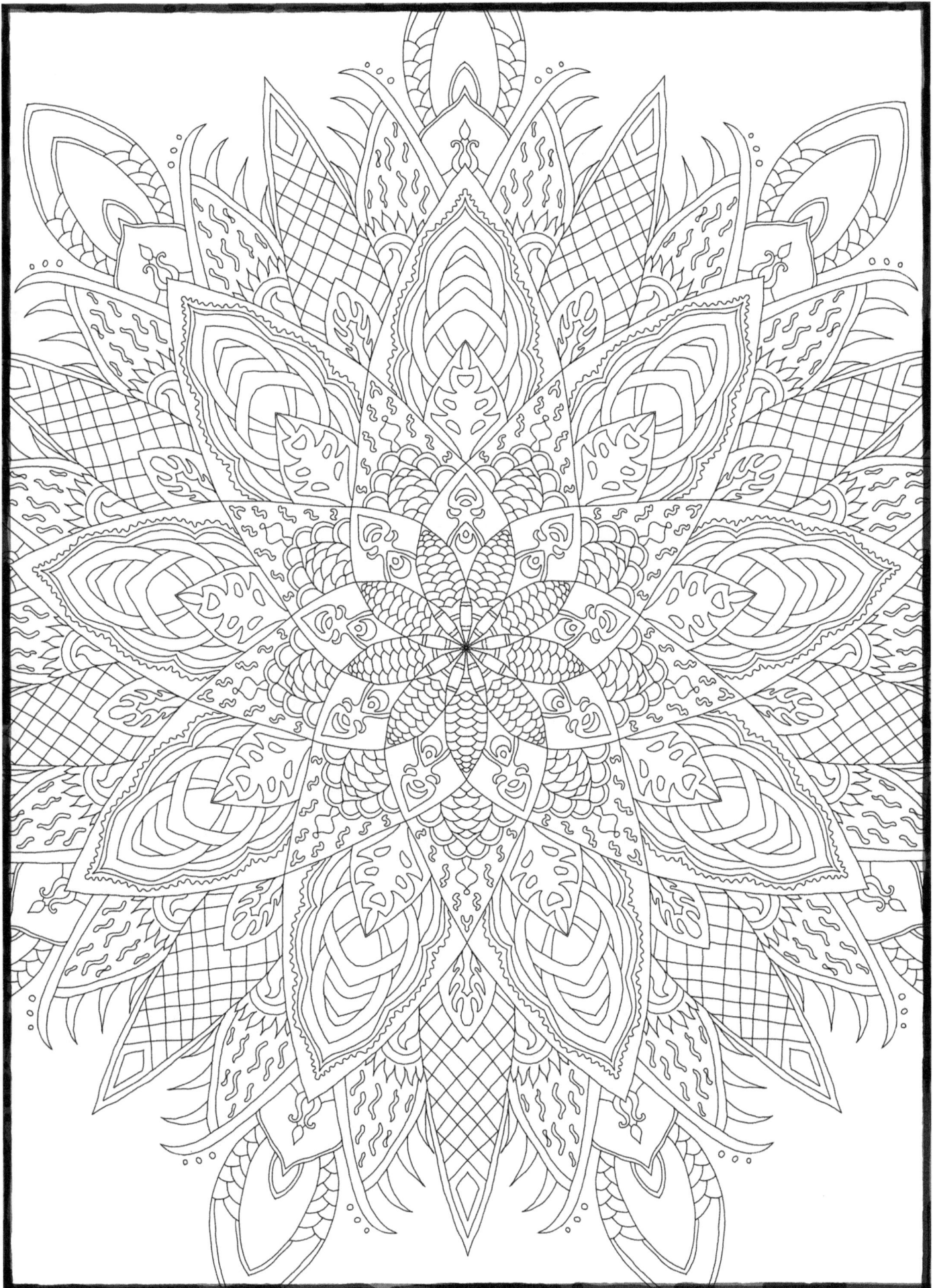

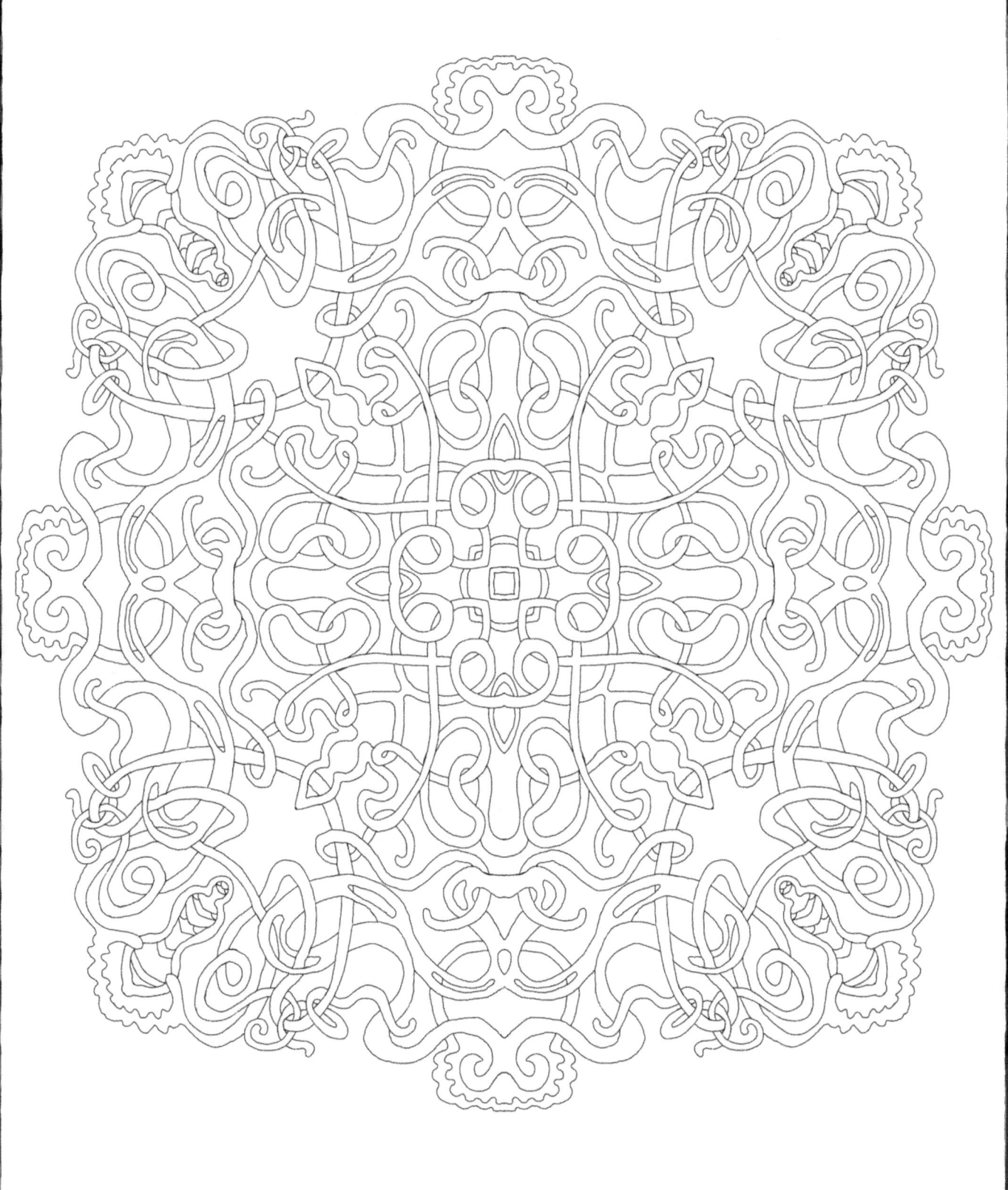

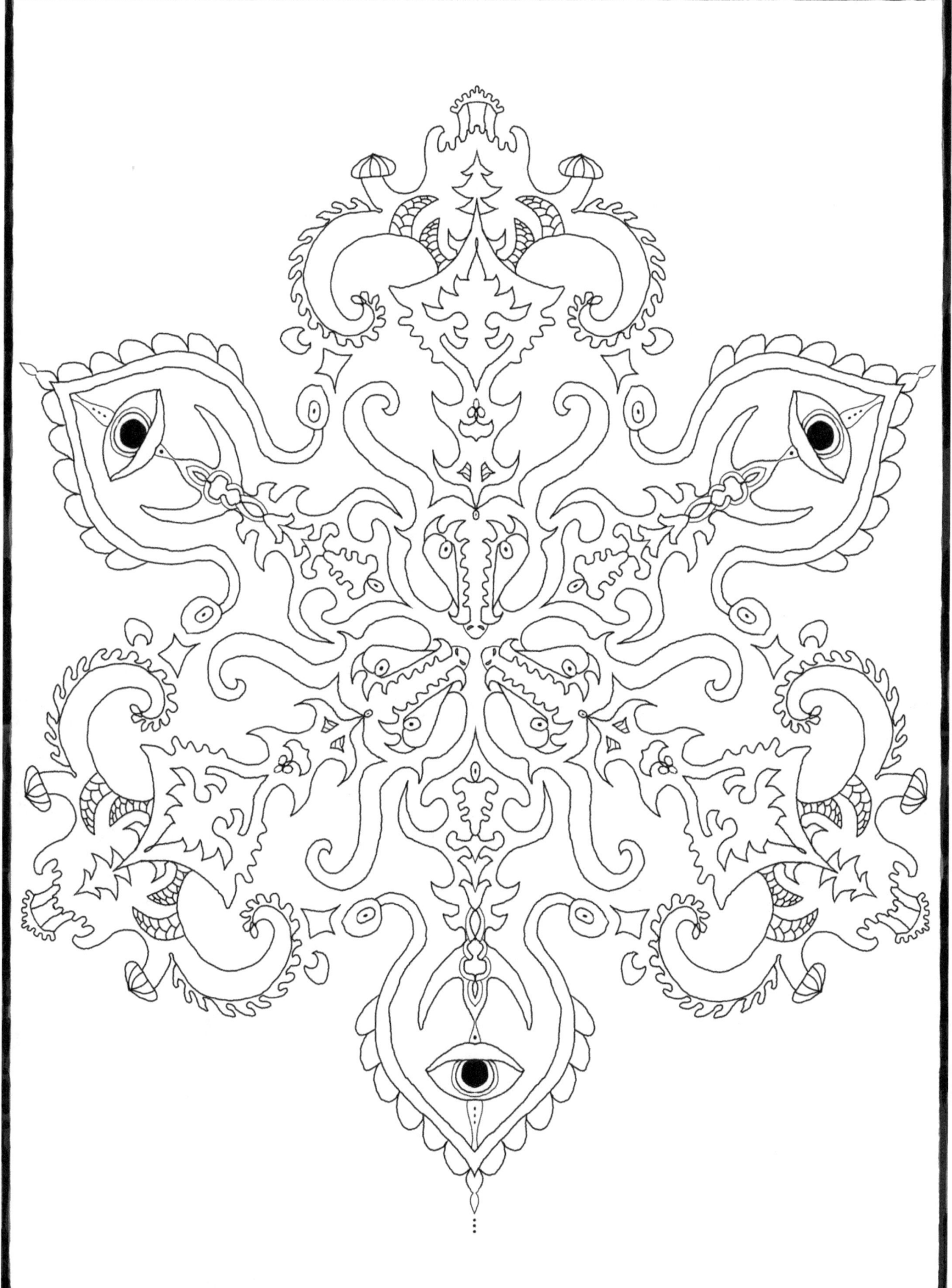

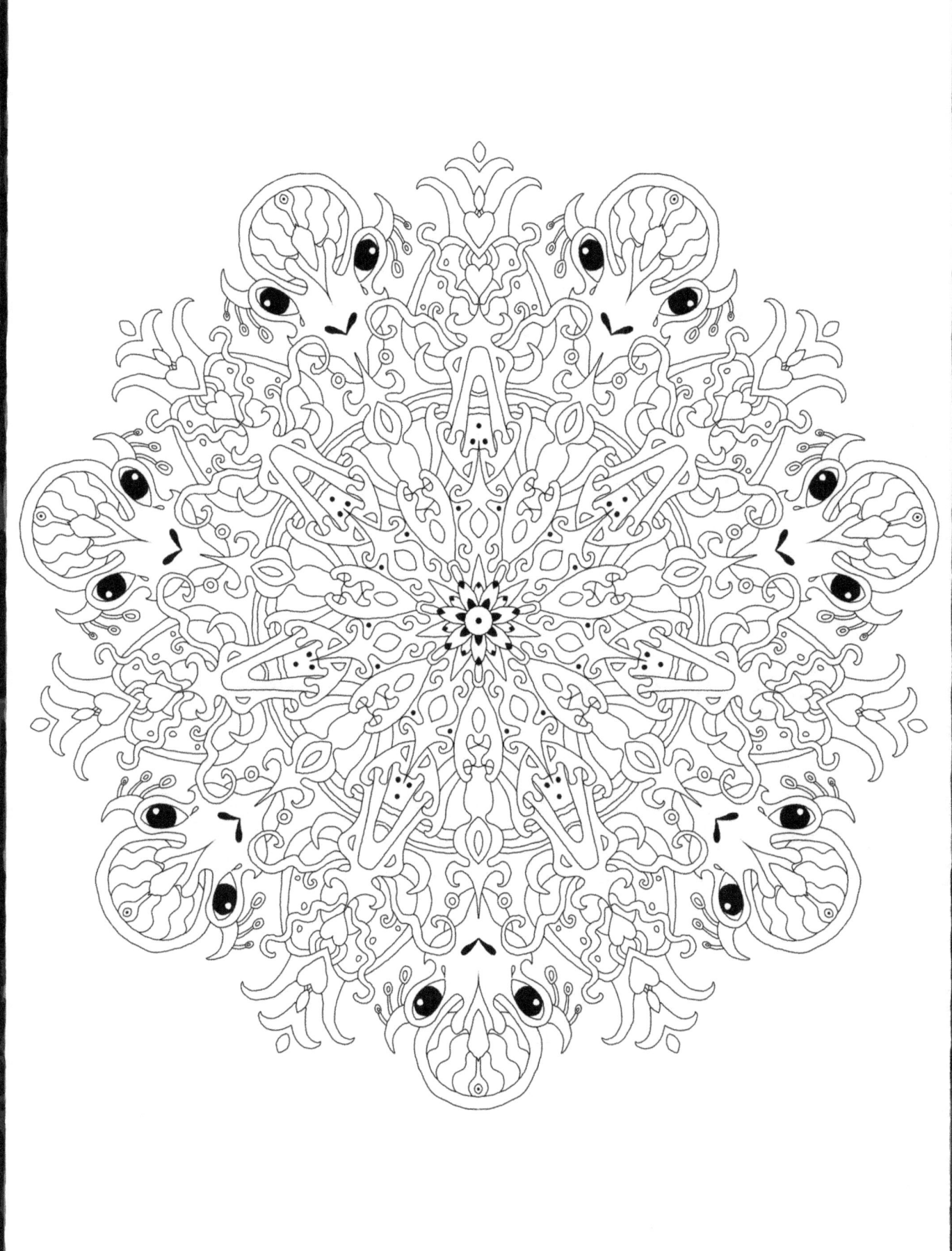

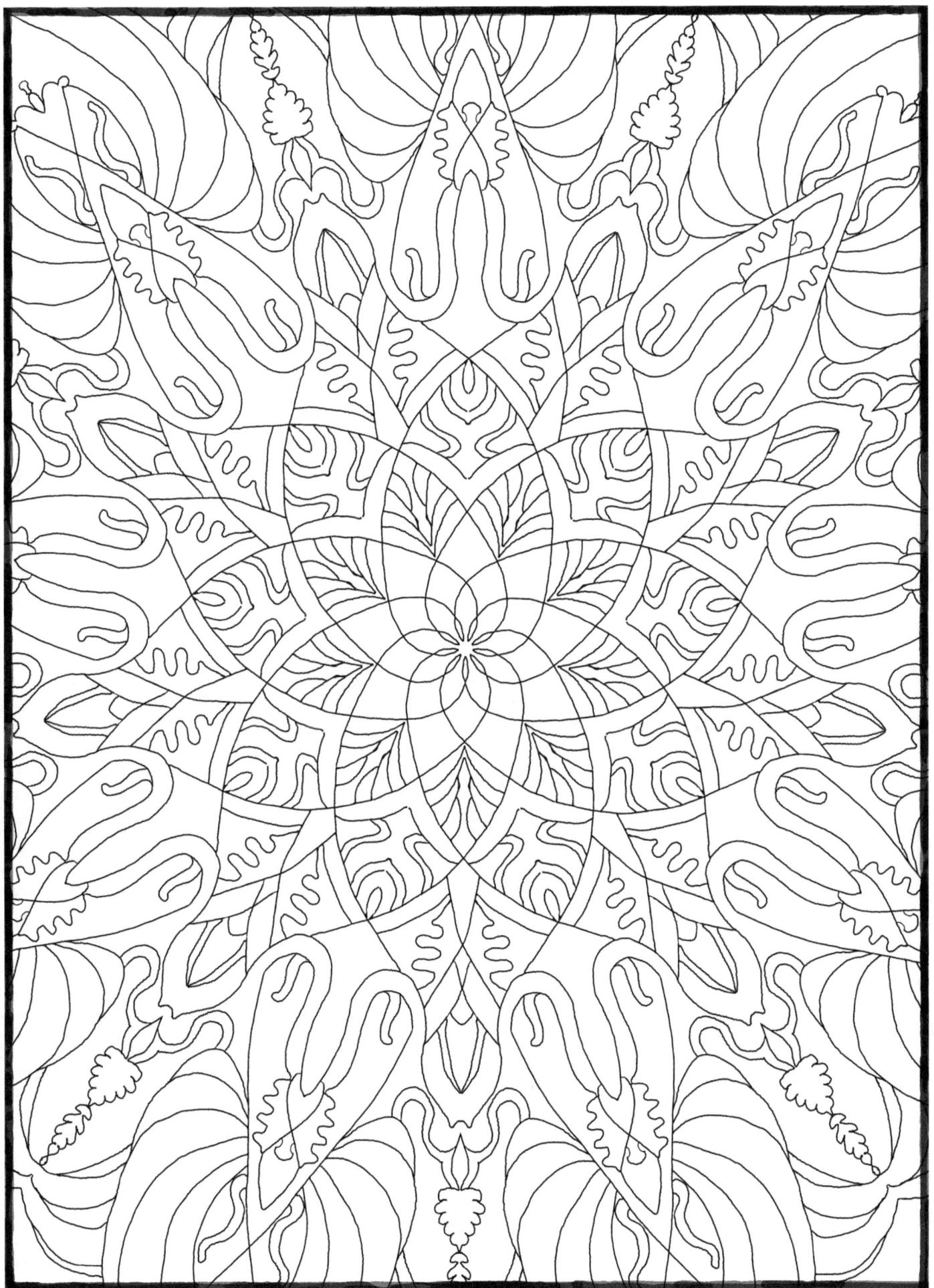

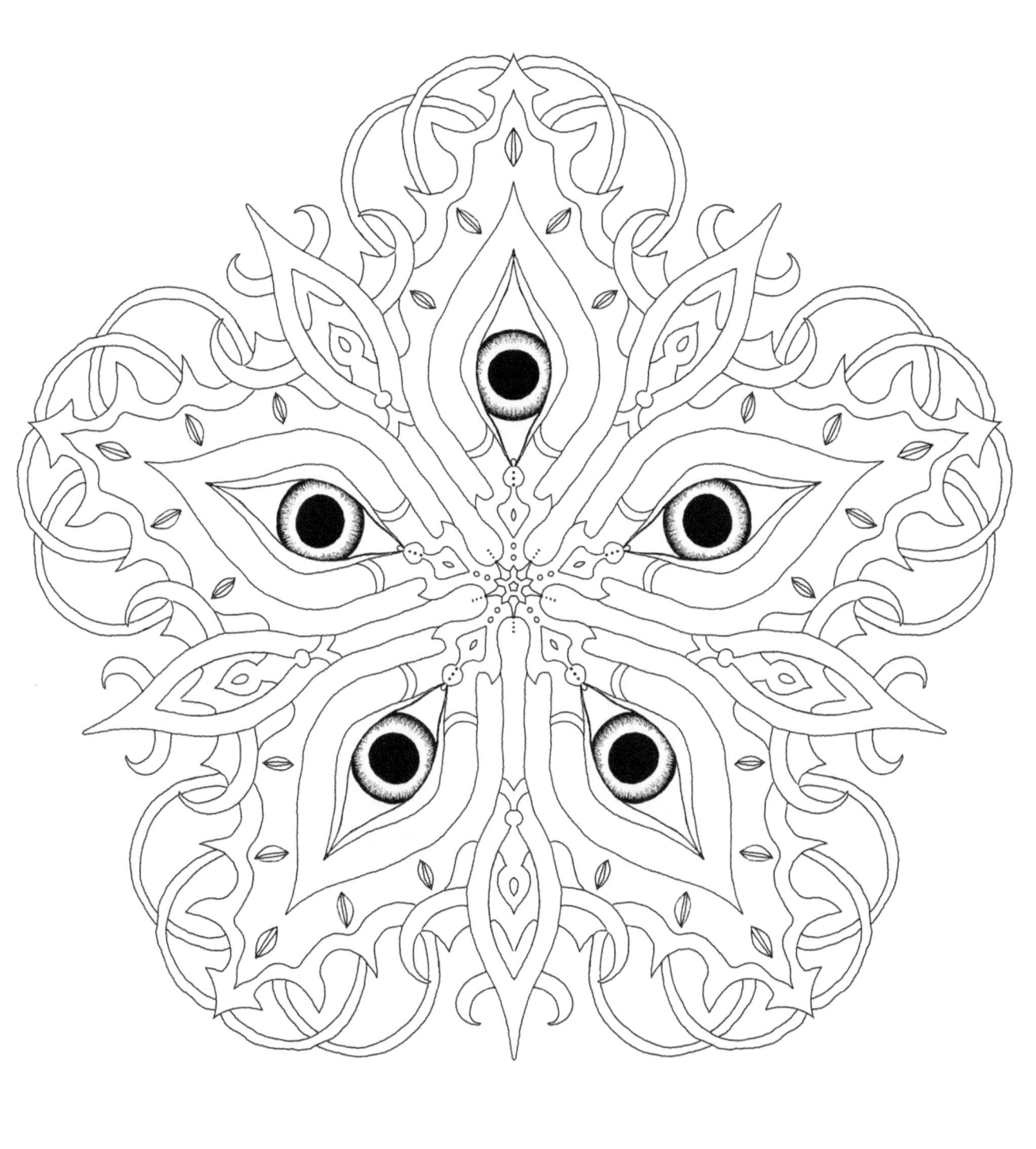

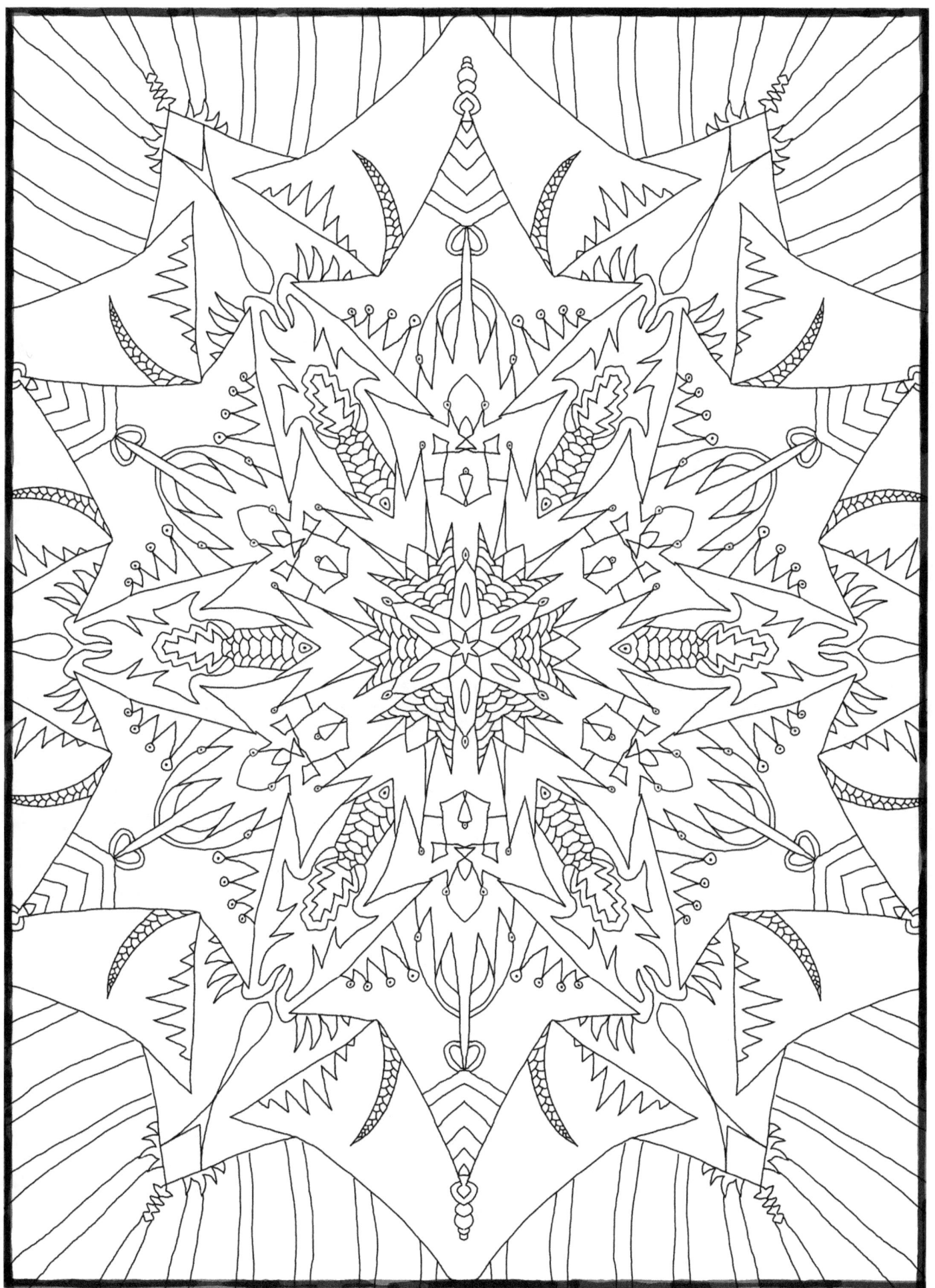

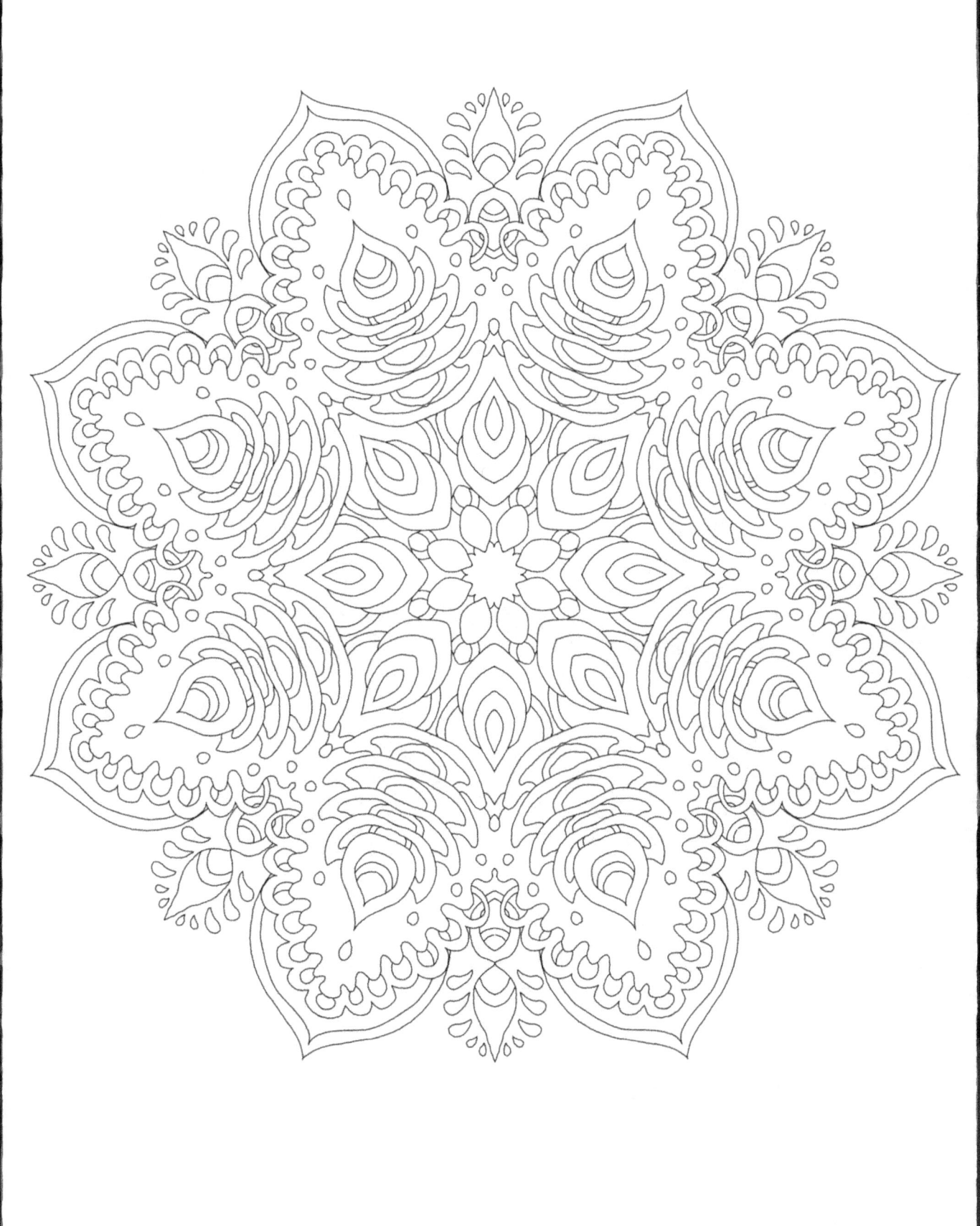

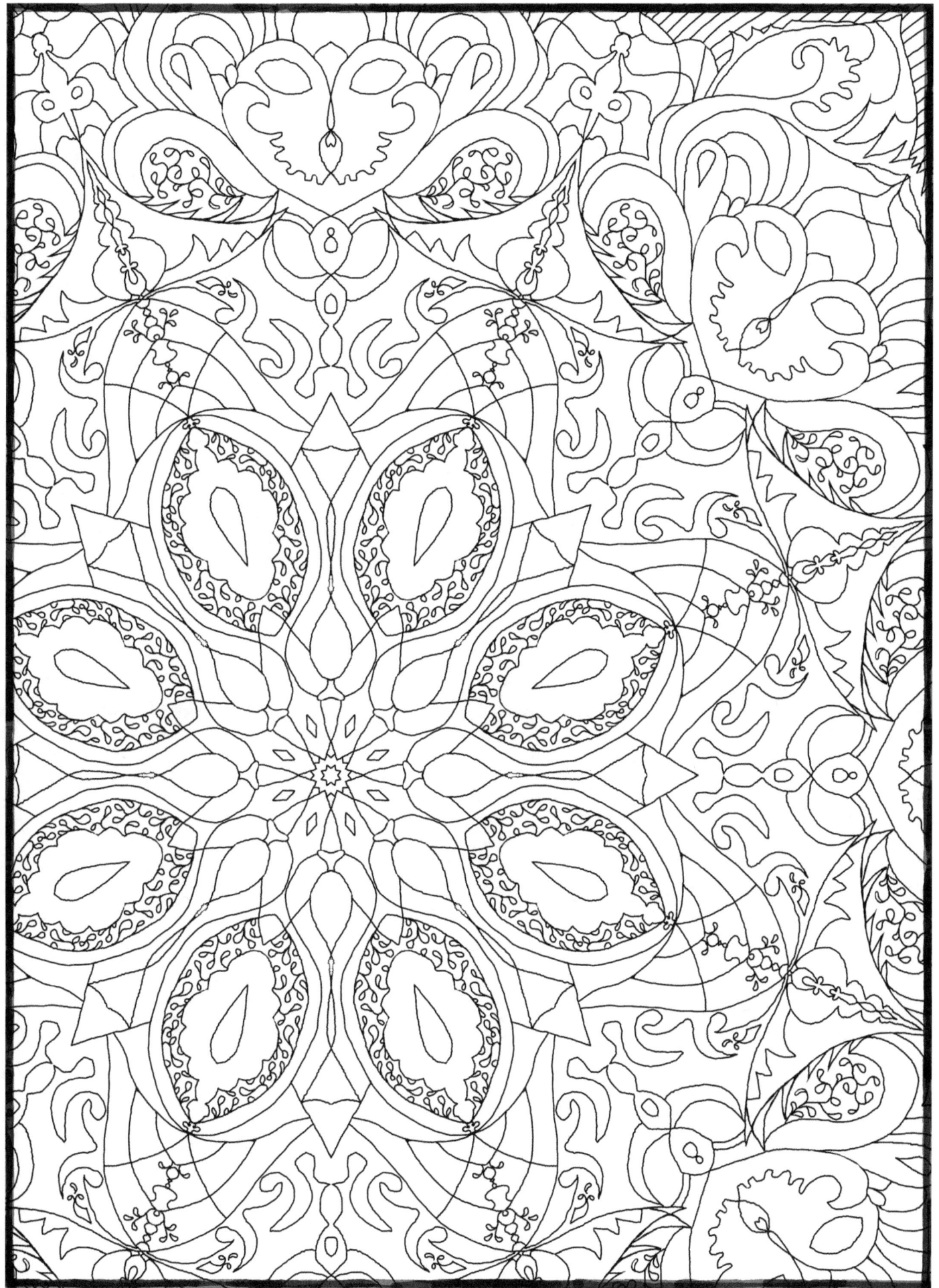

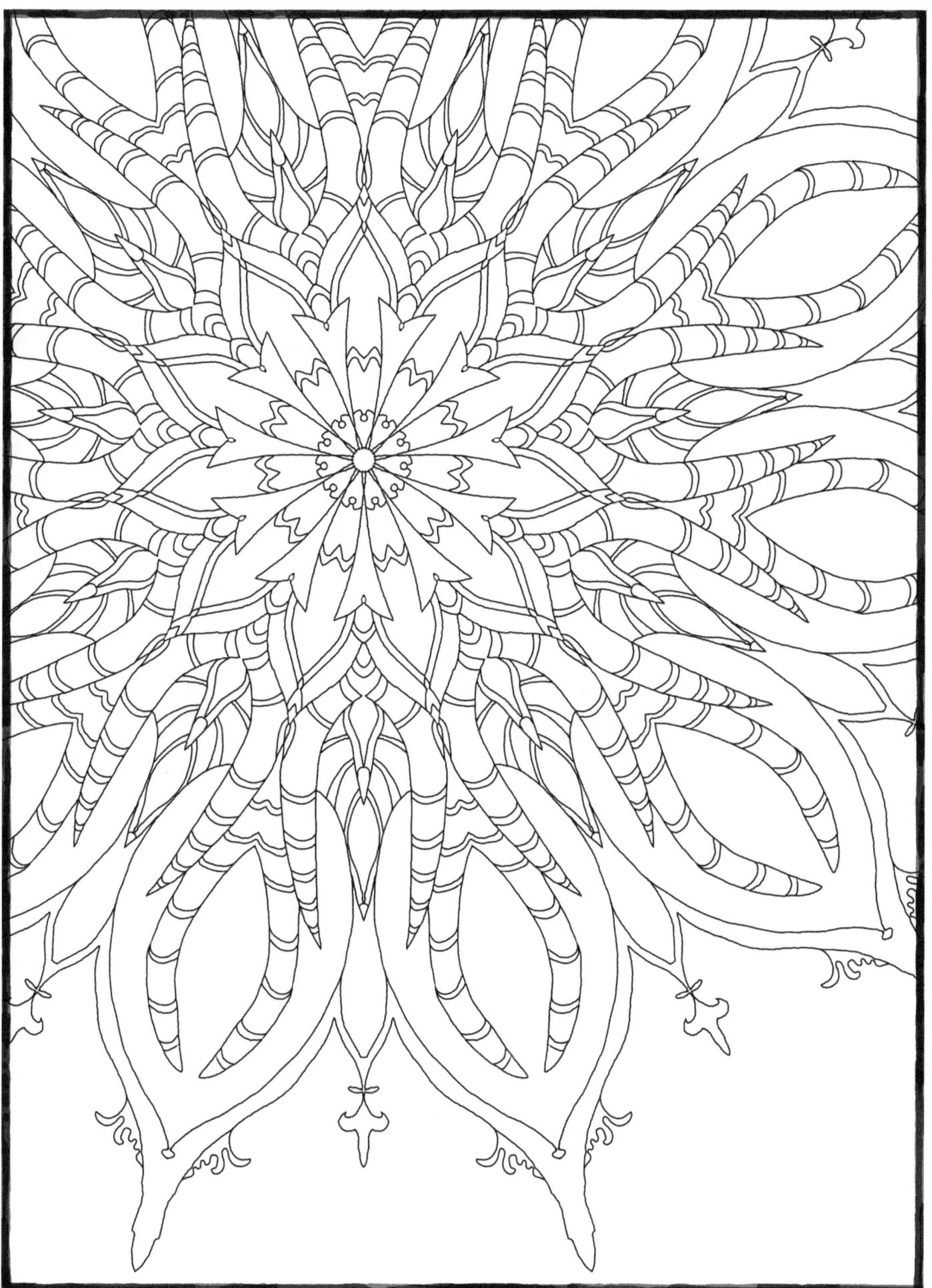

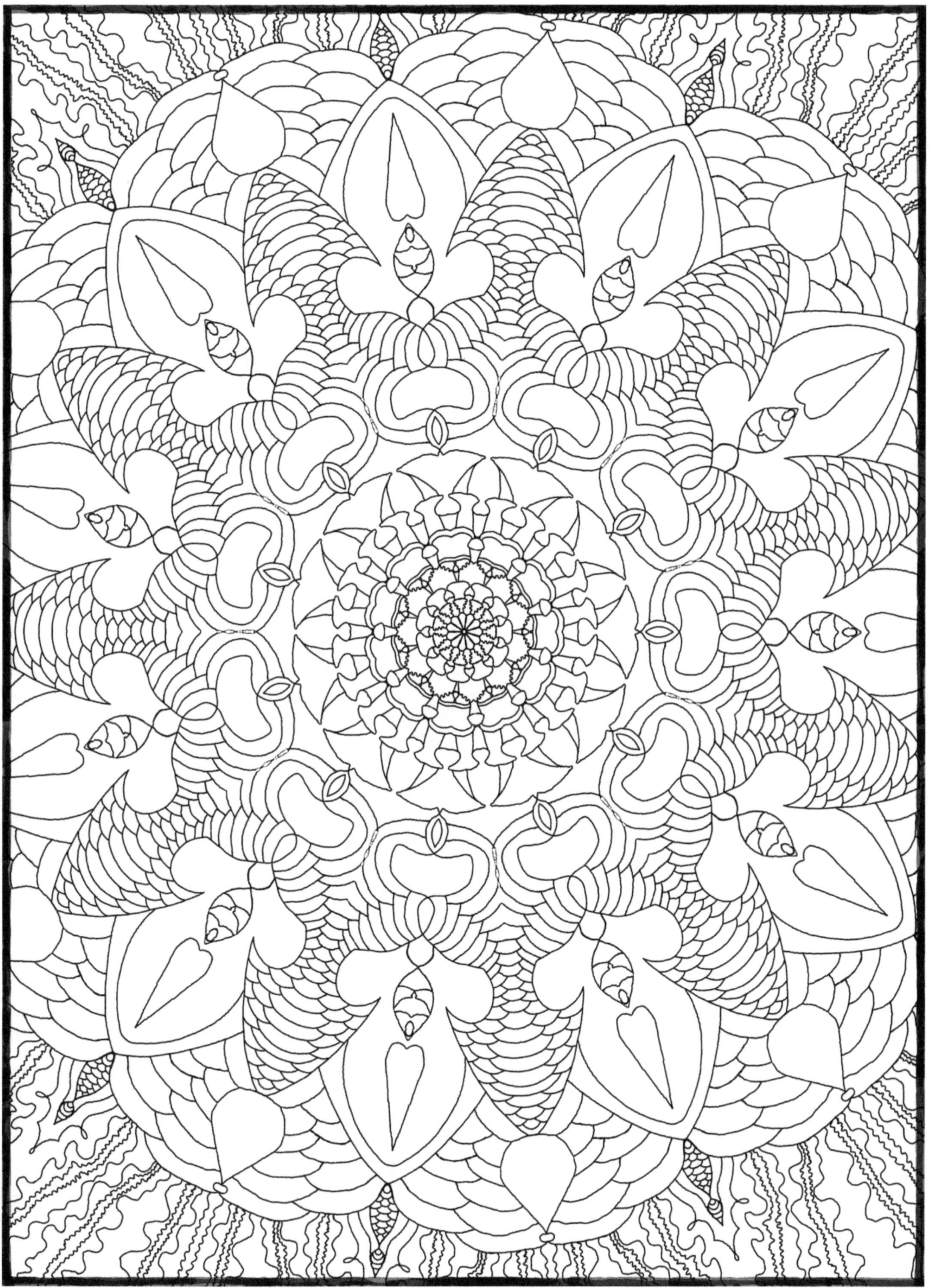

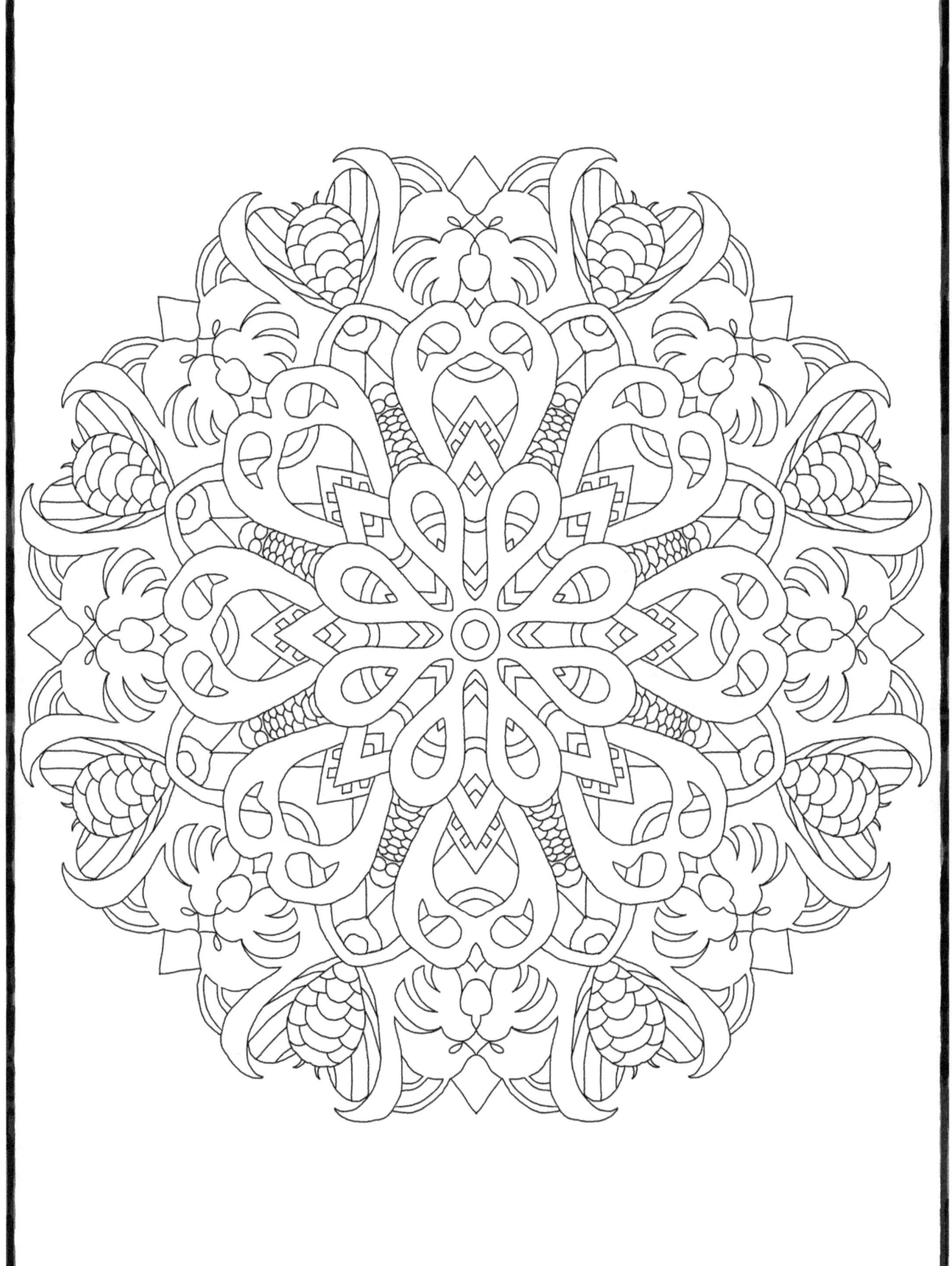

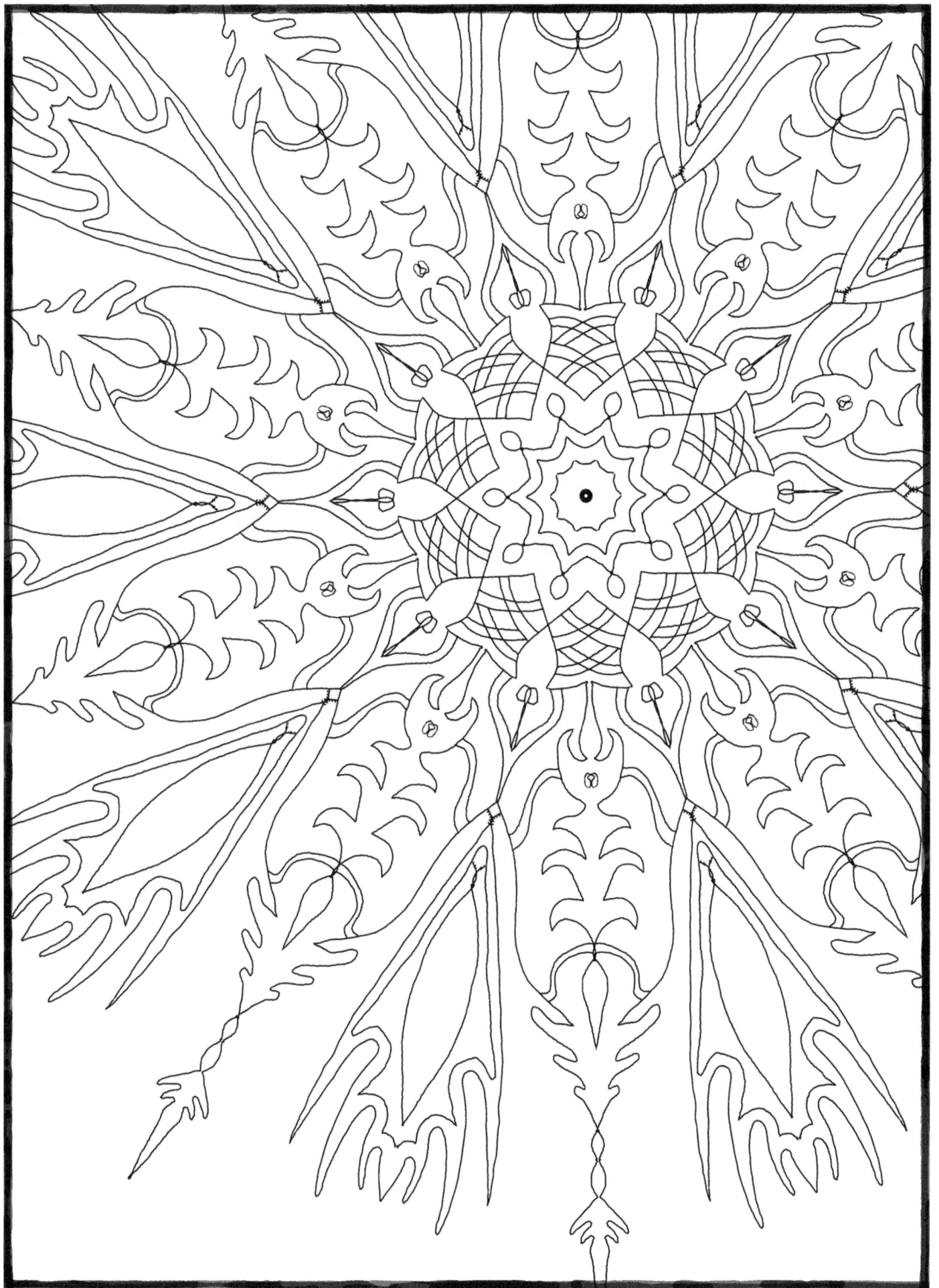

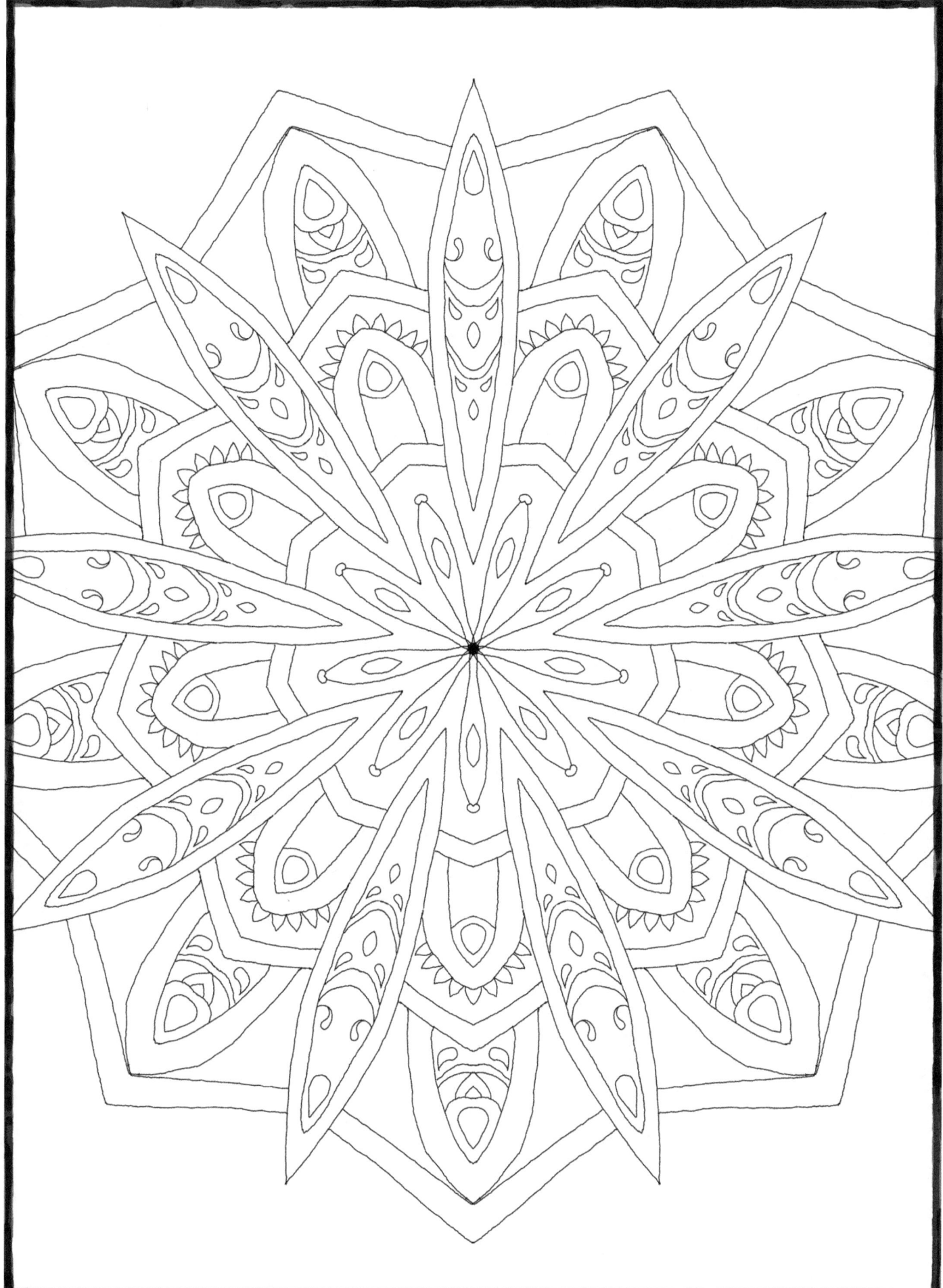

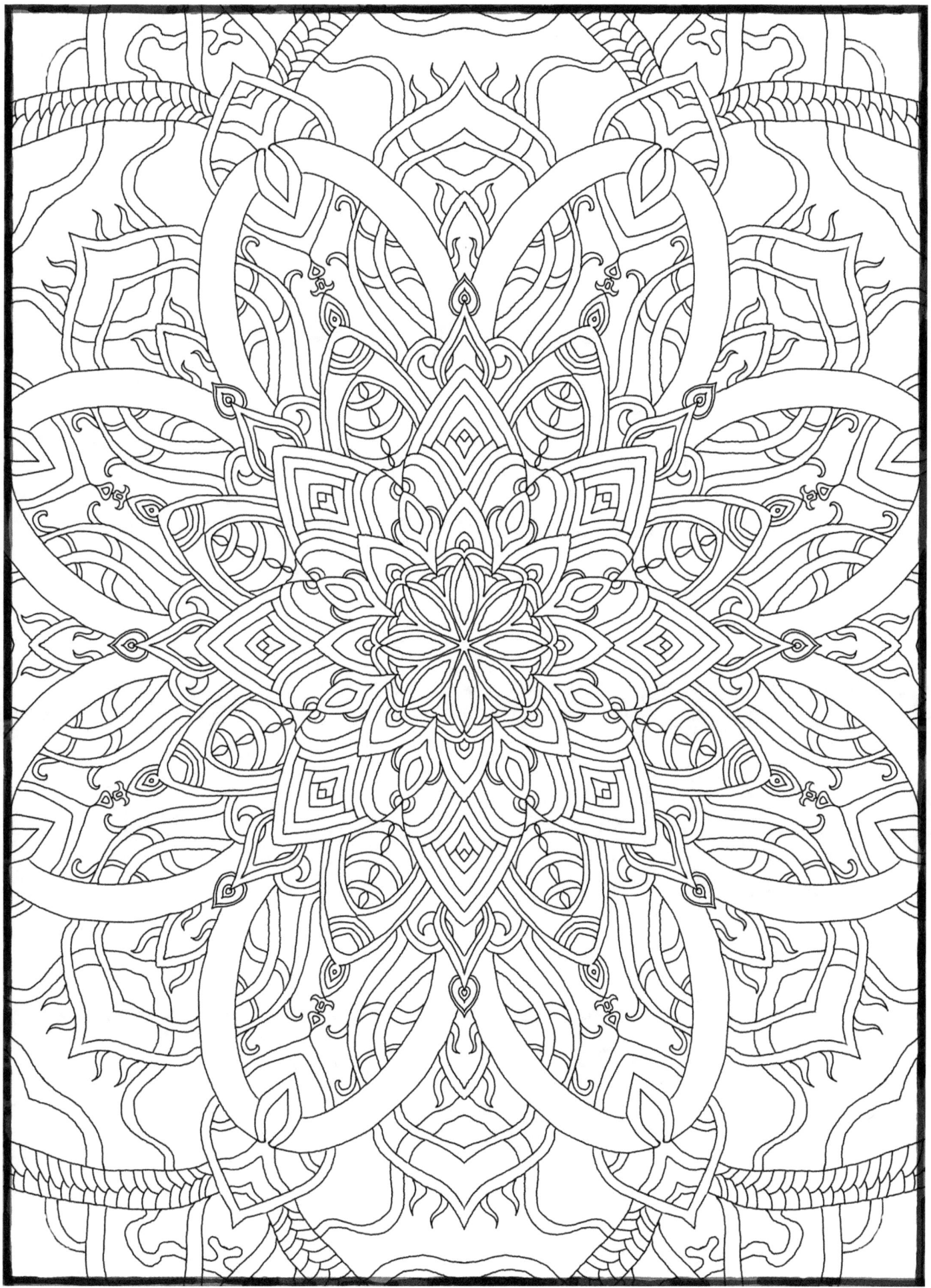

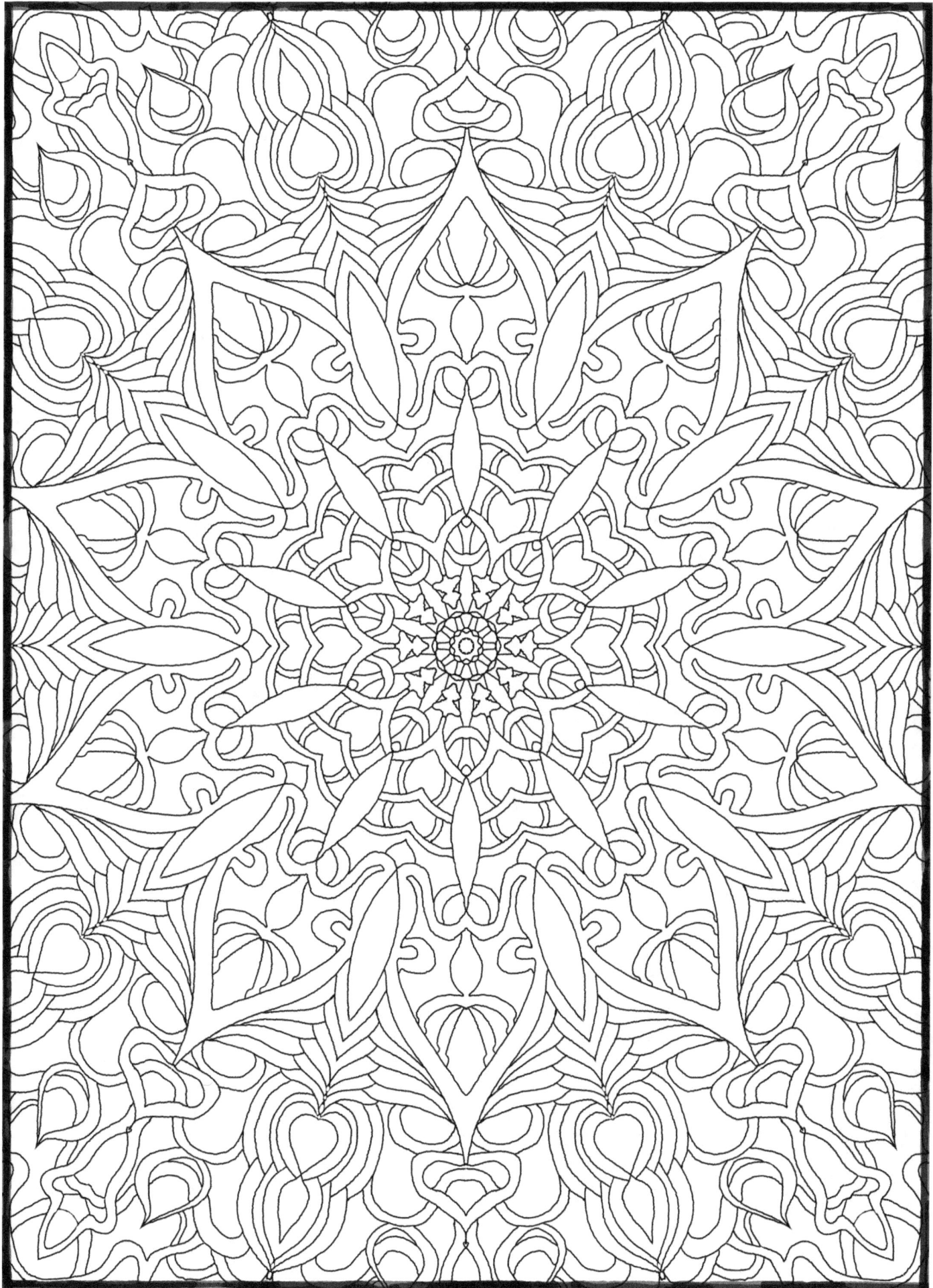

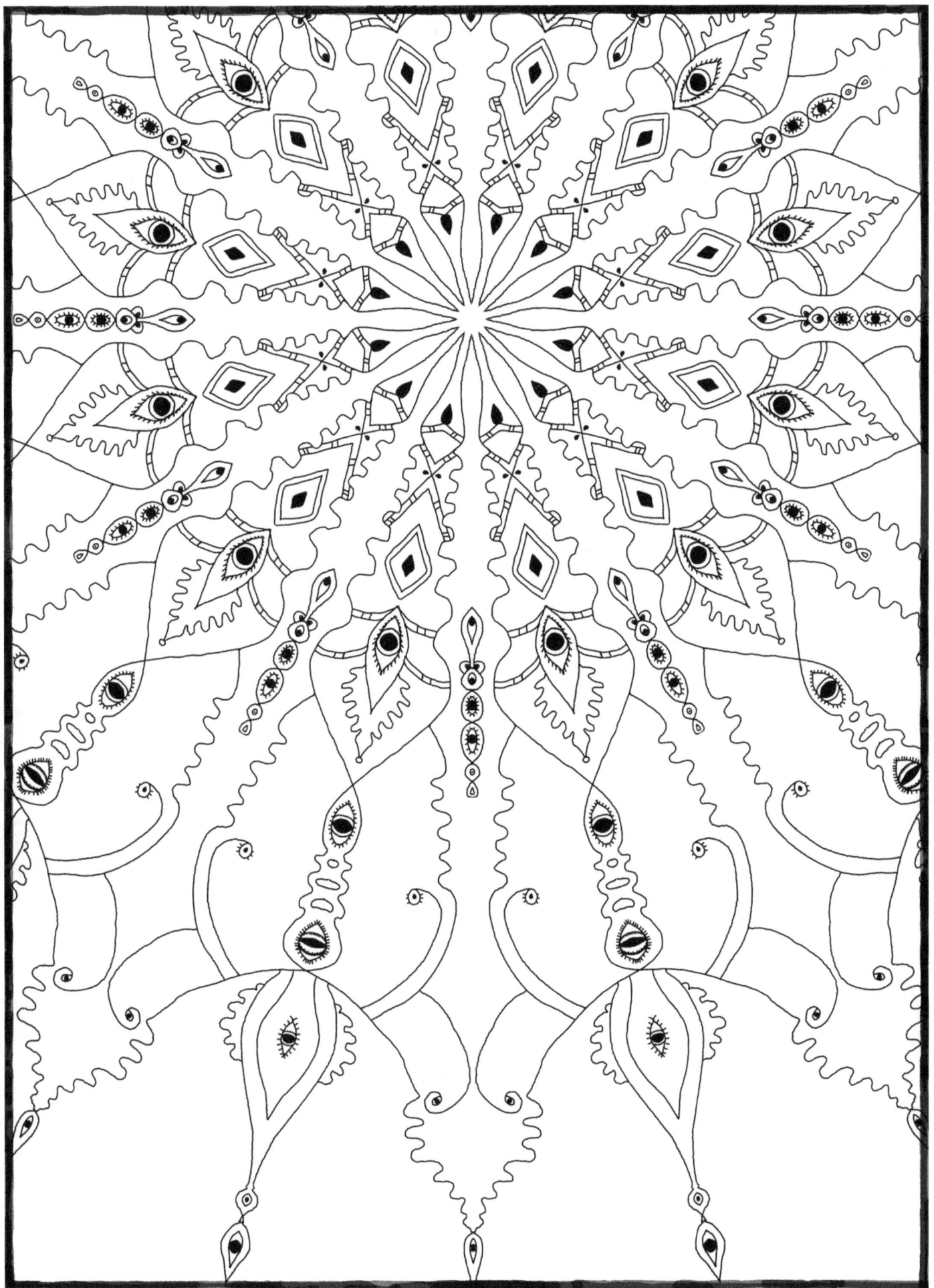

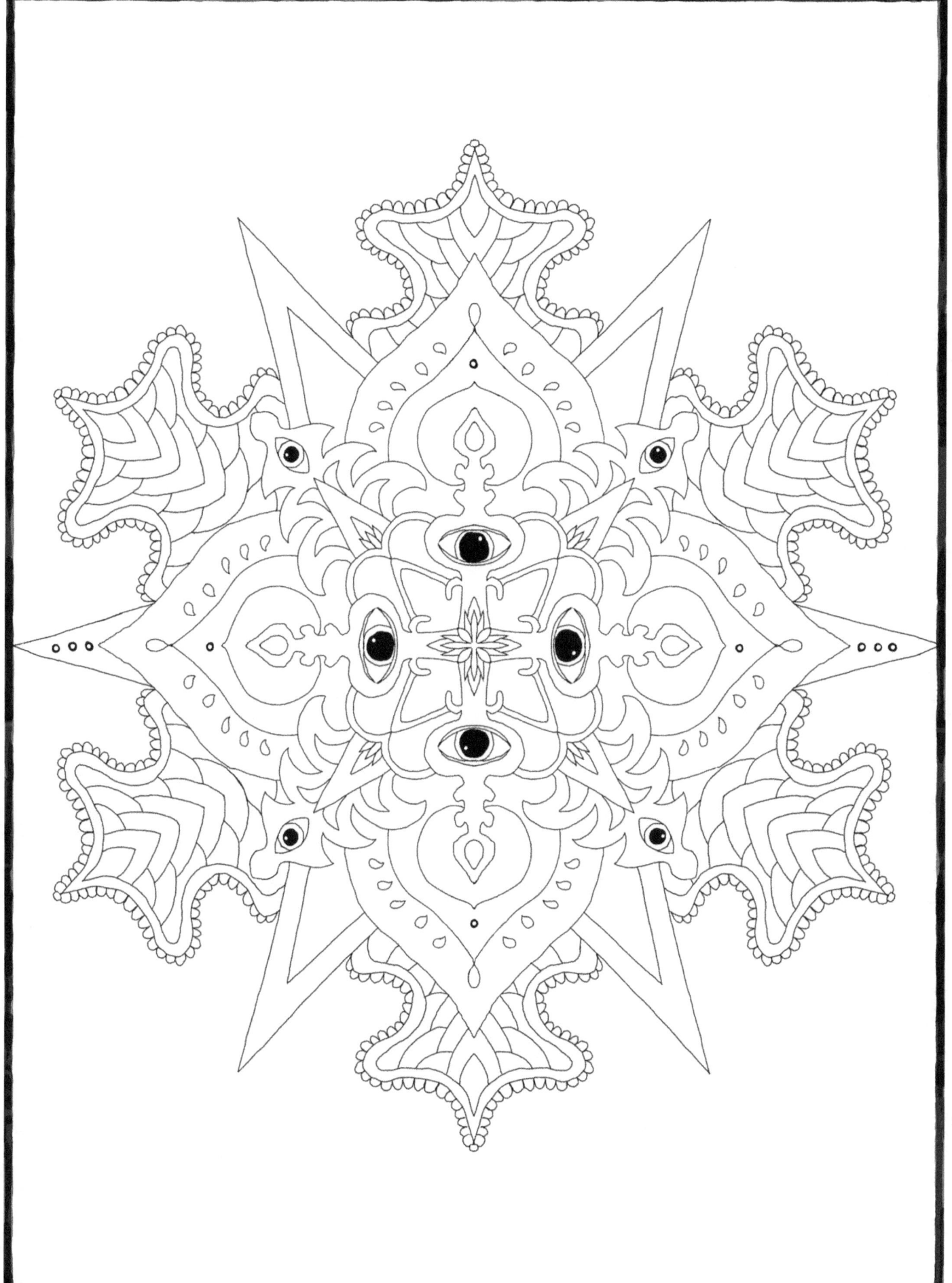

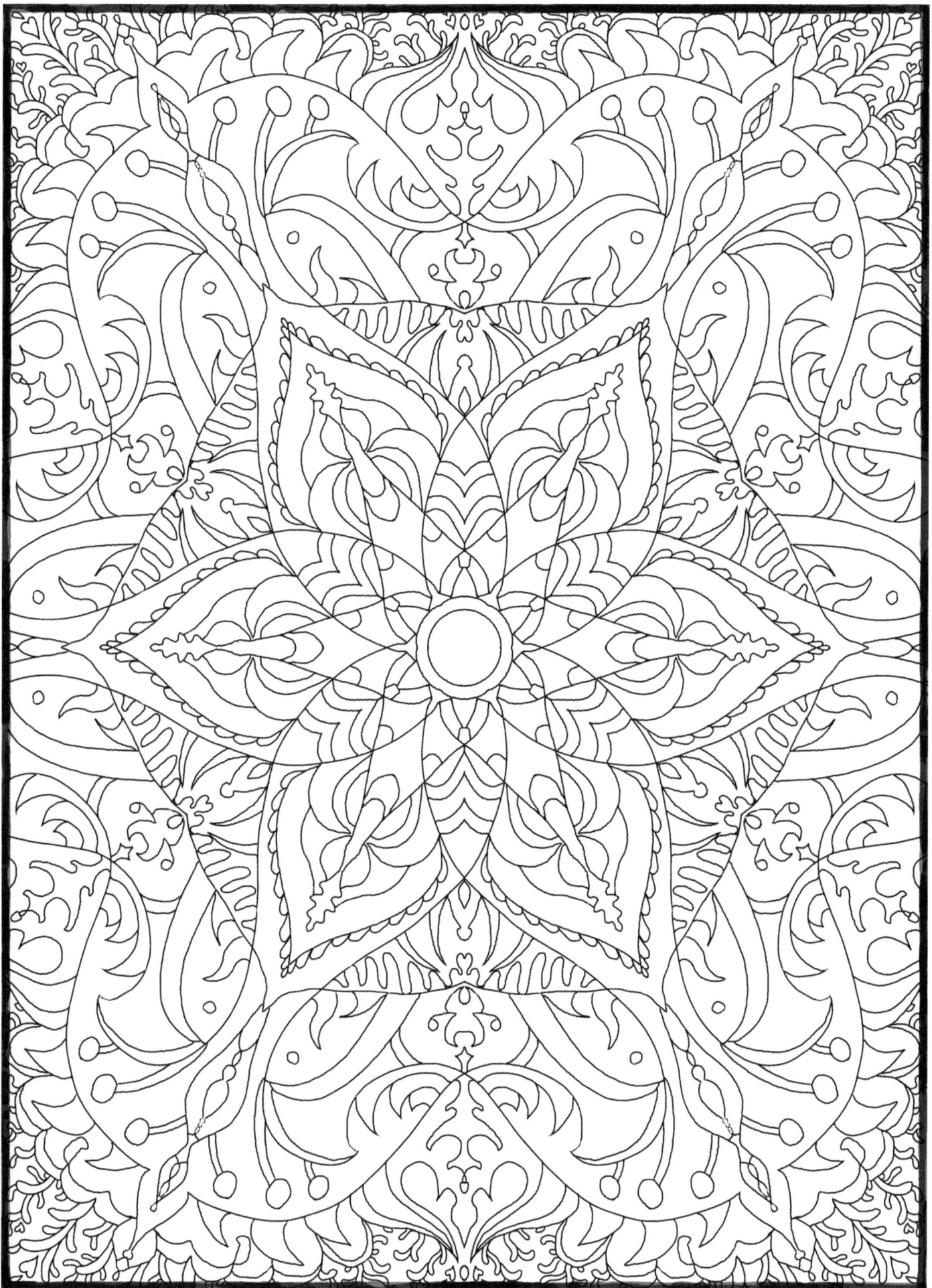

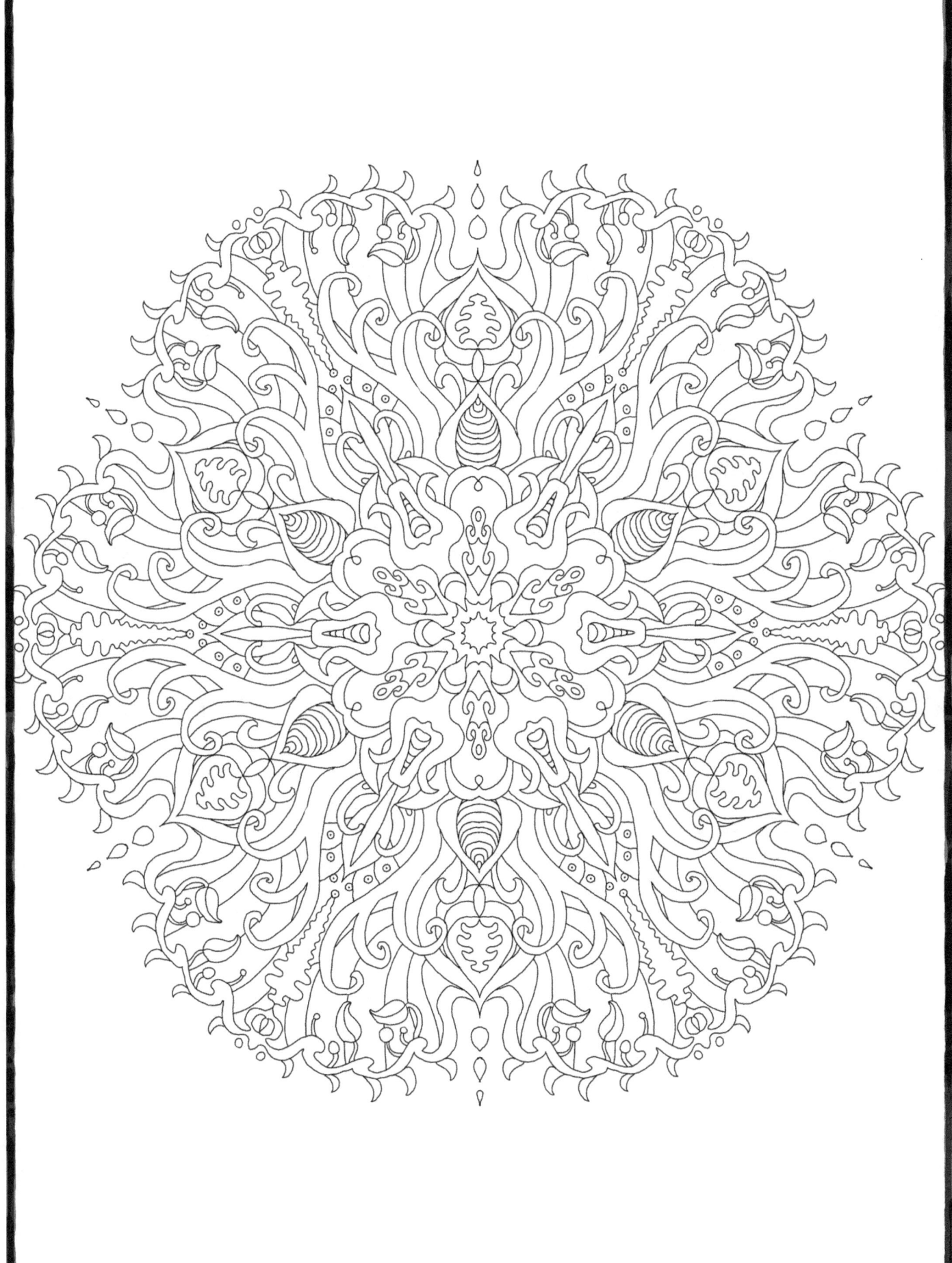

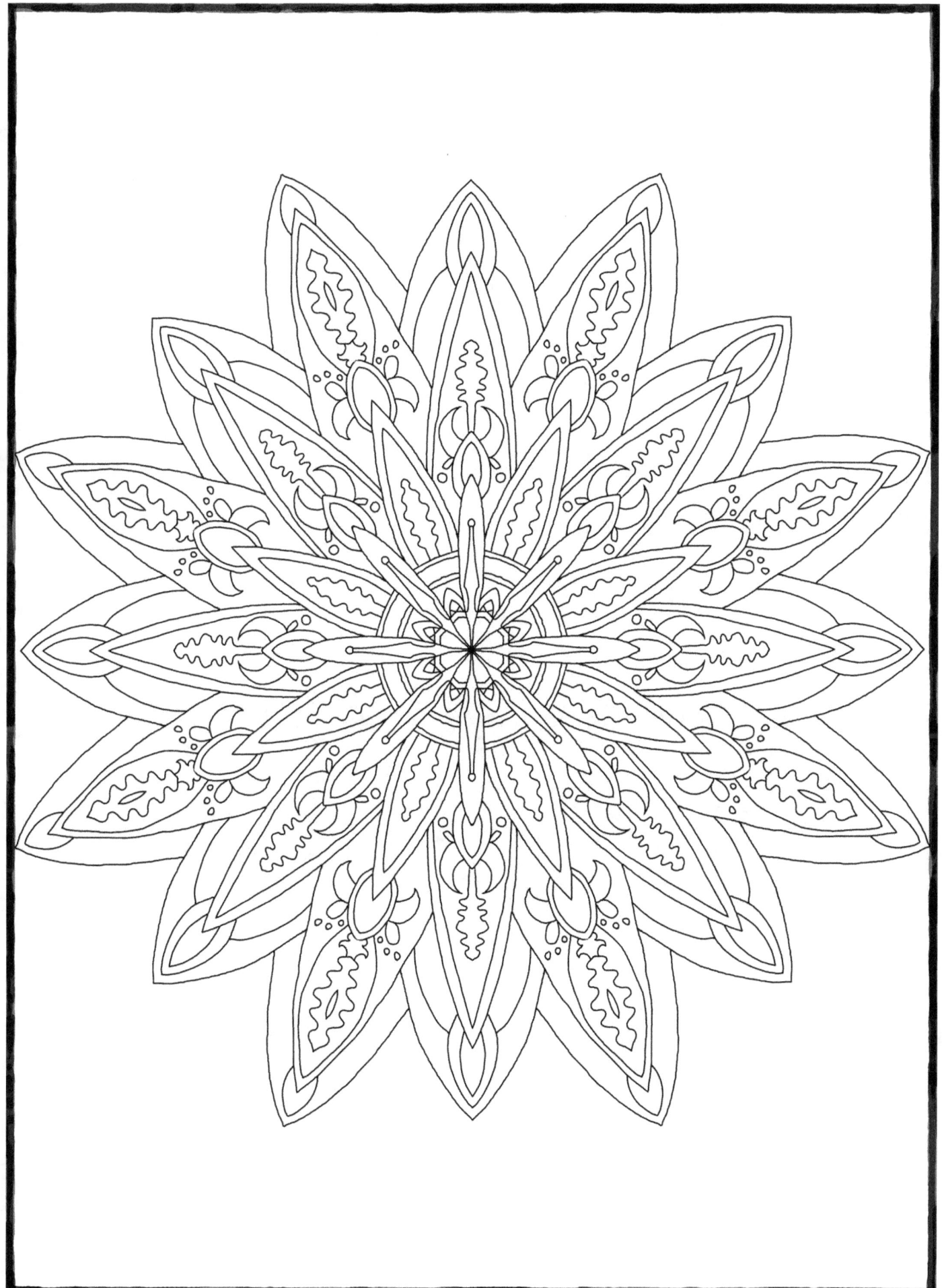

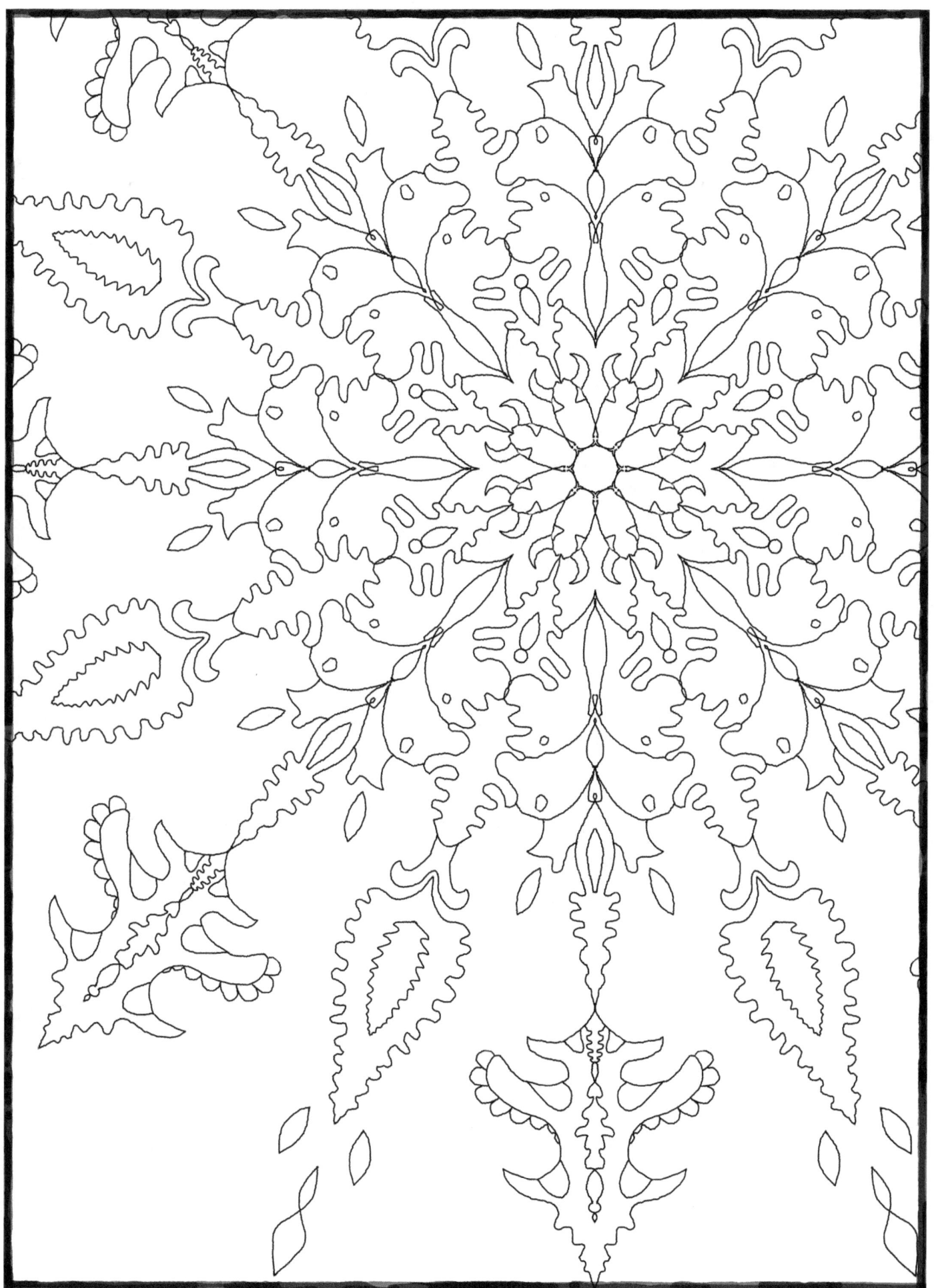

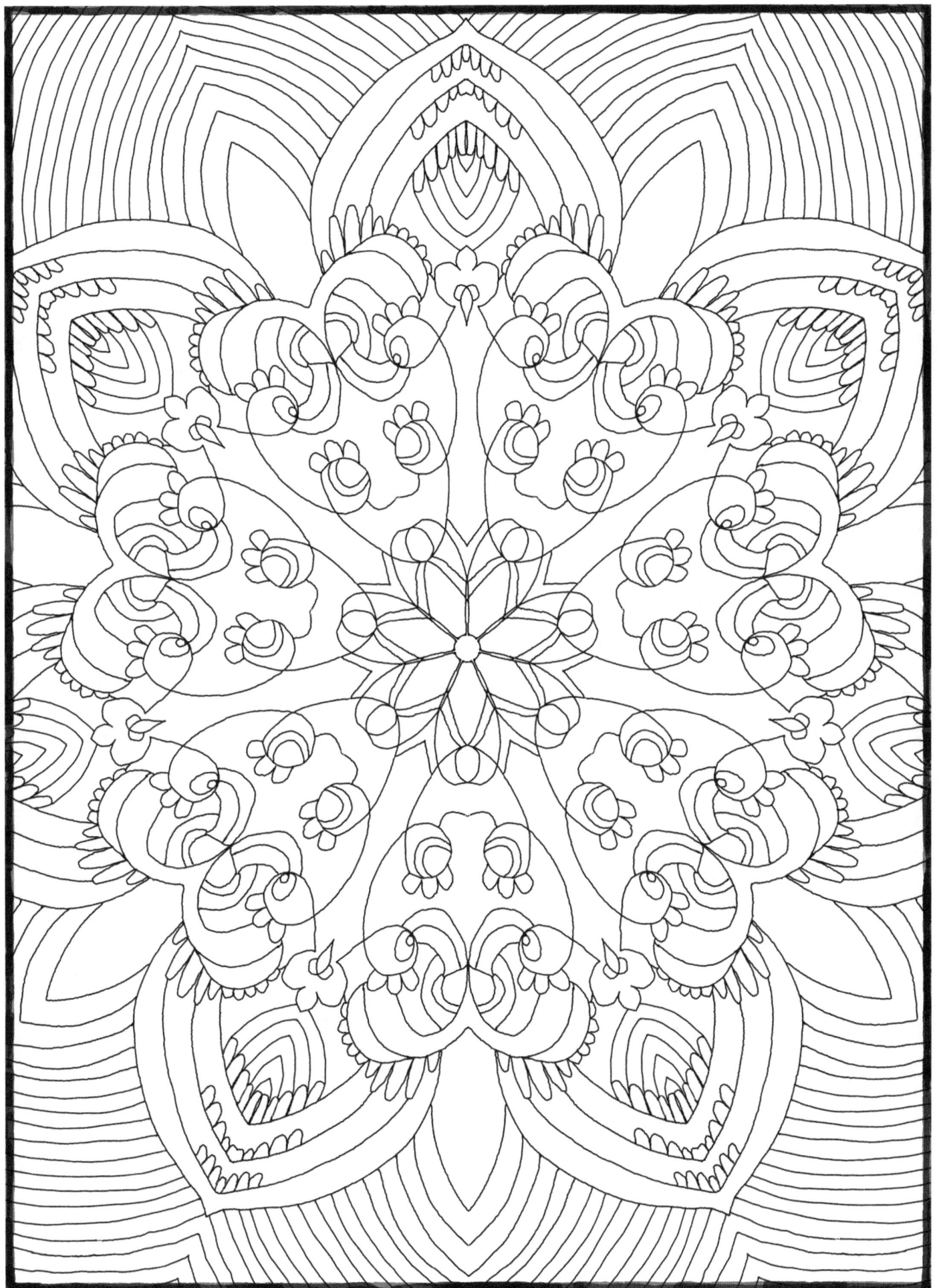

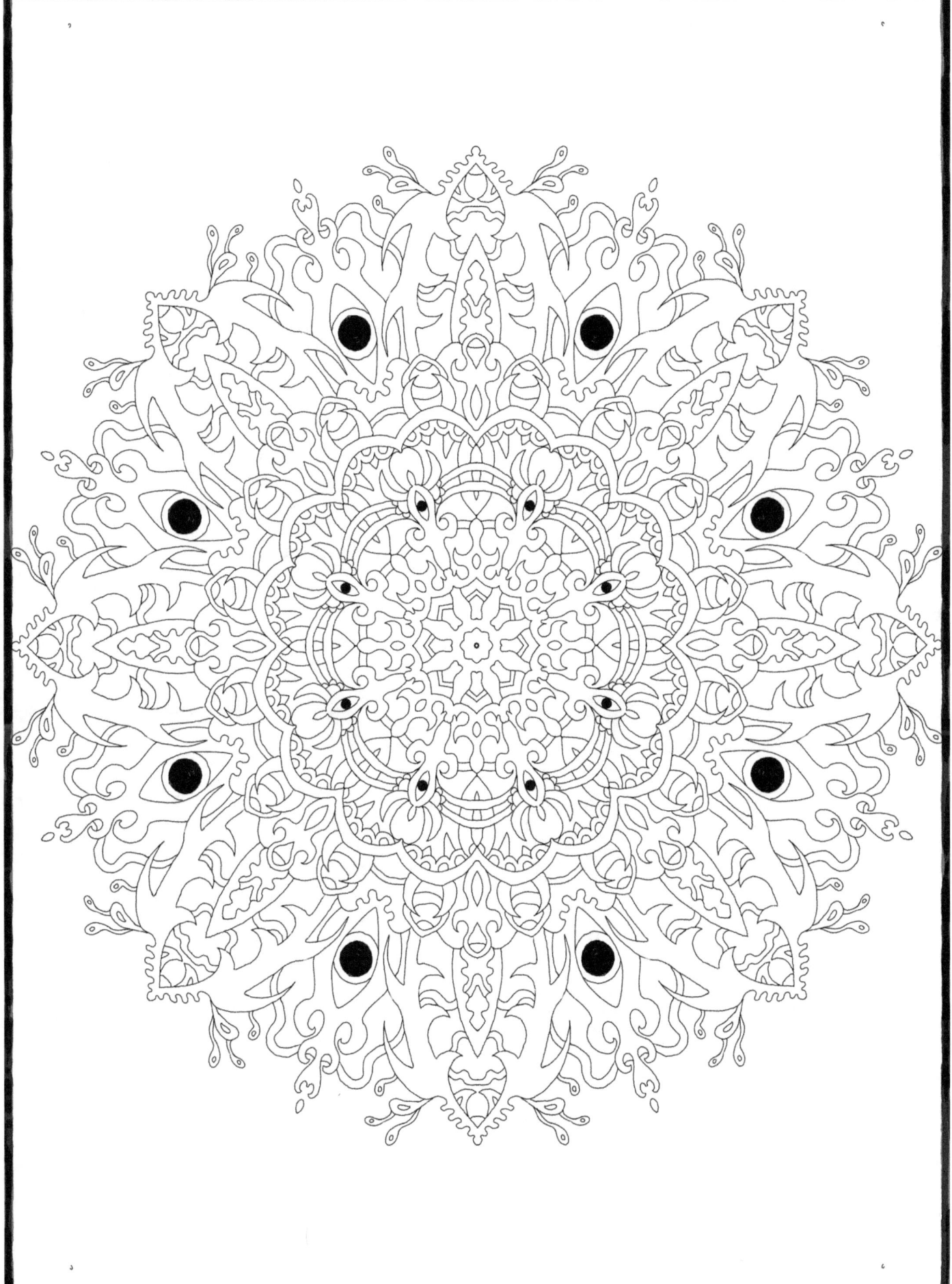

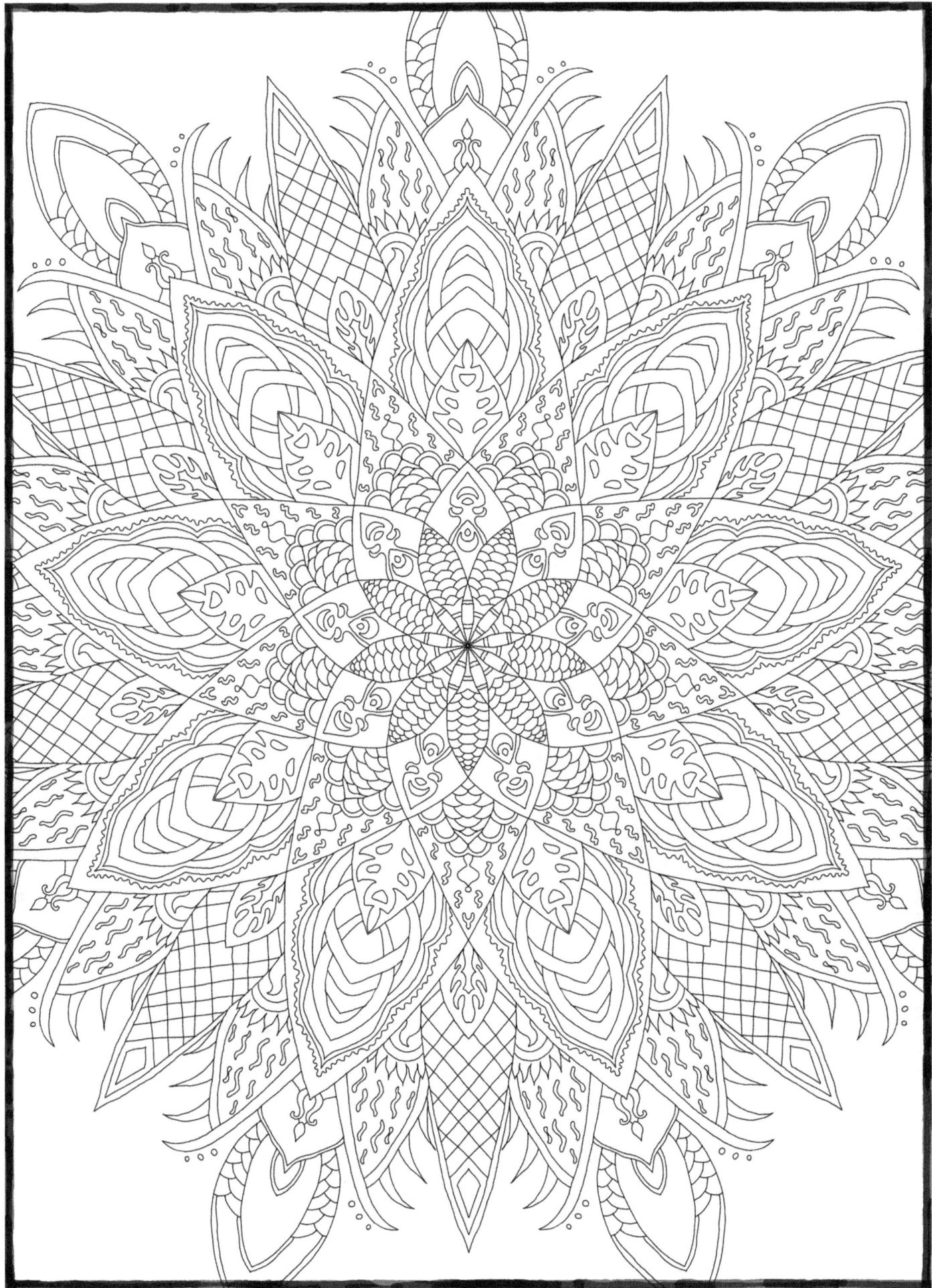

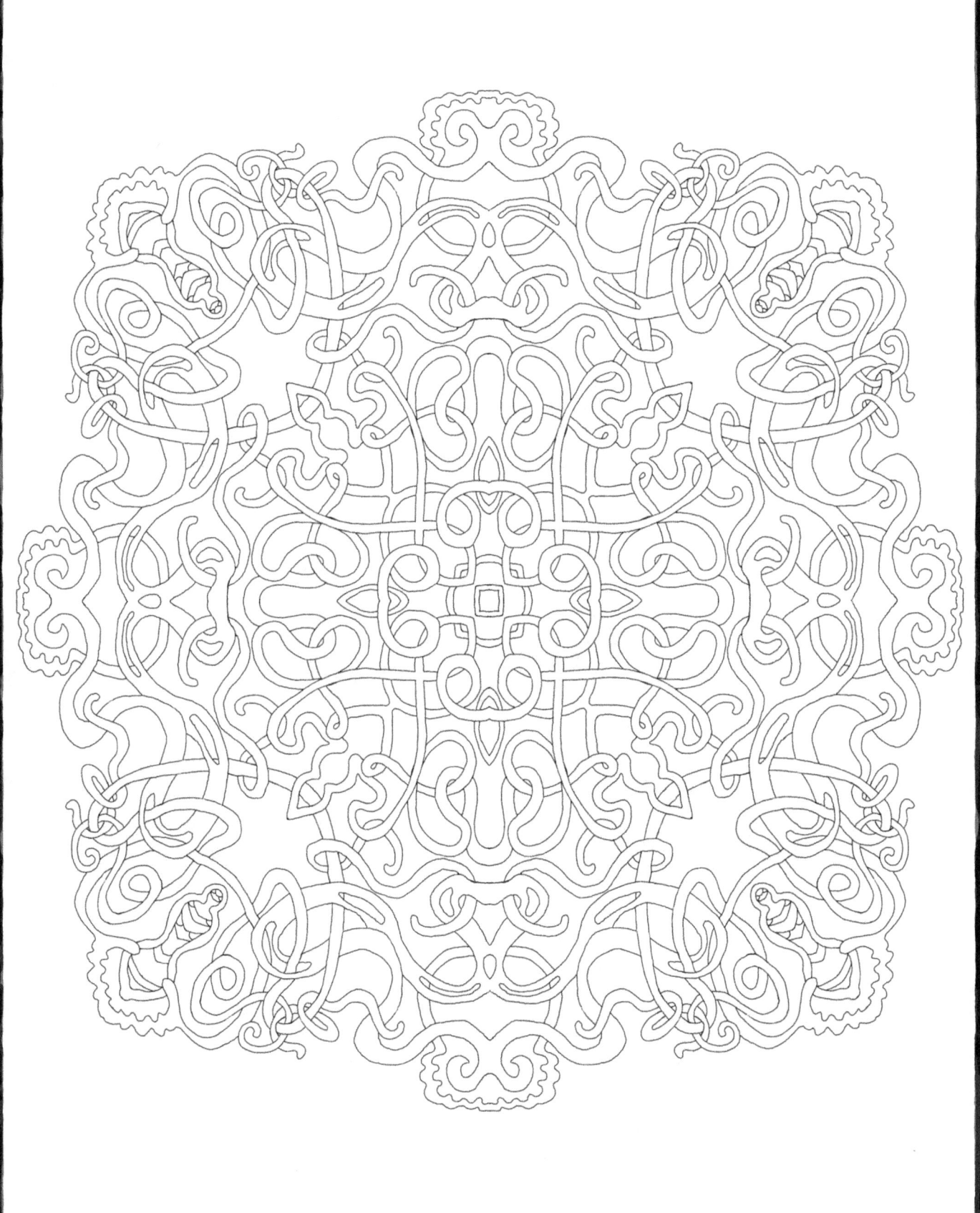

73.

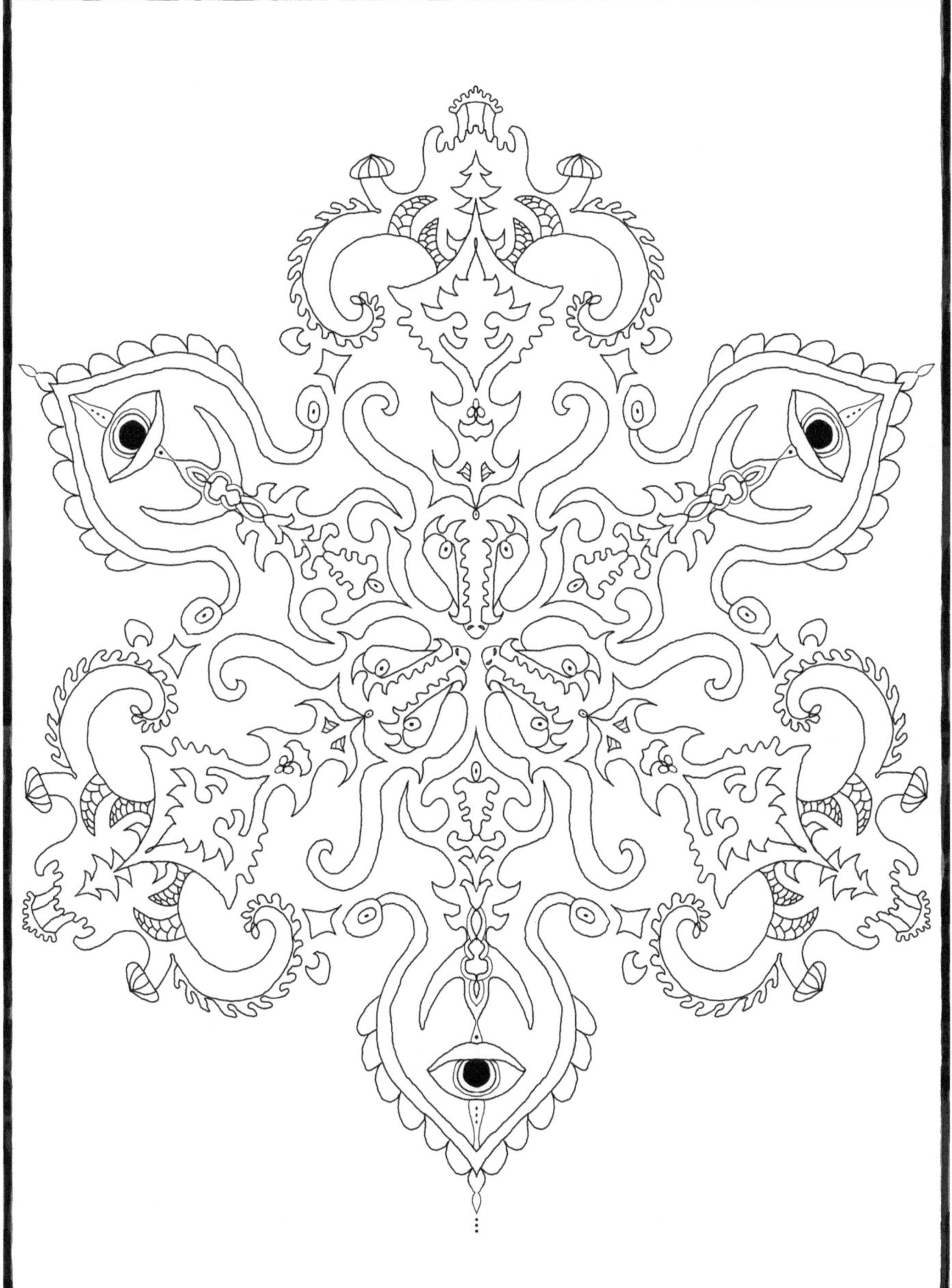

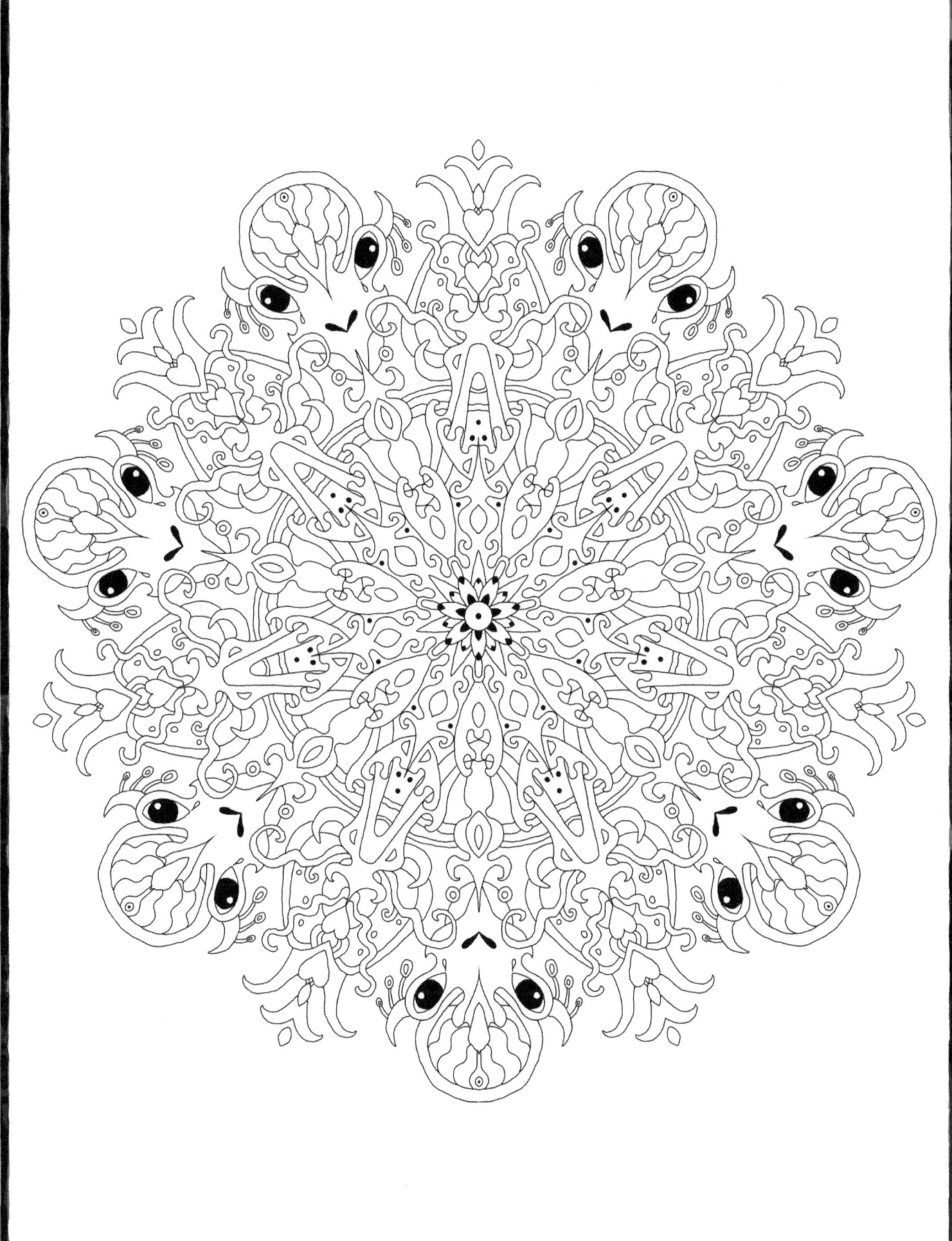

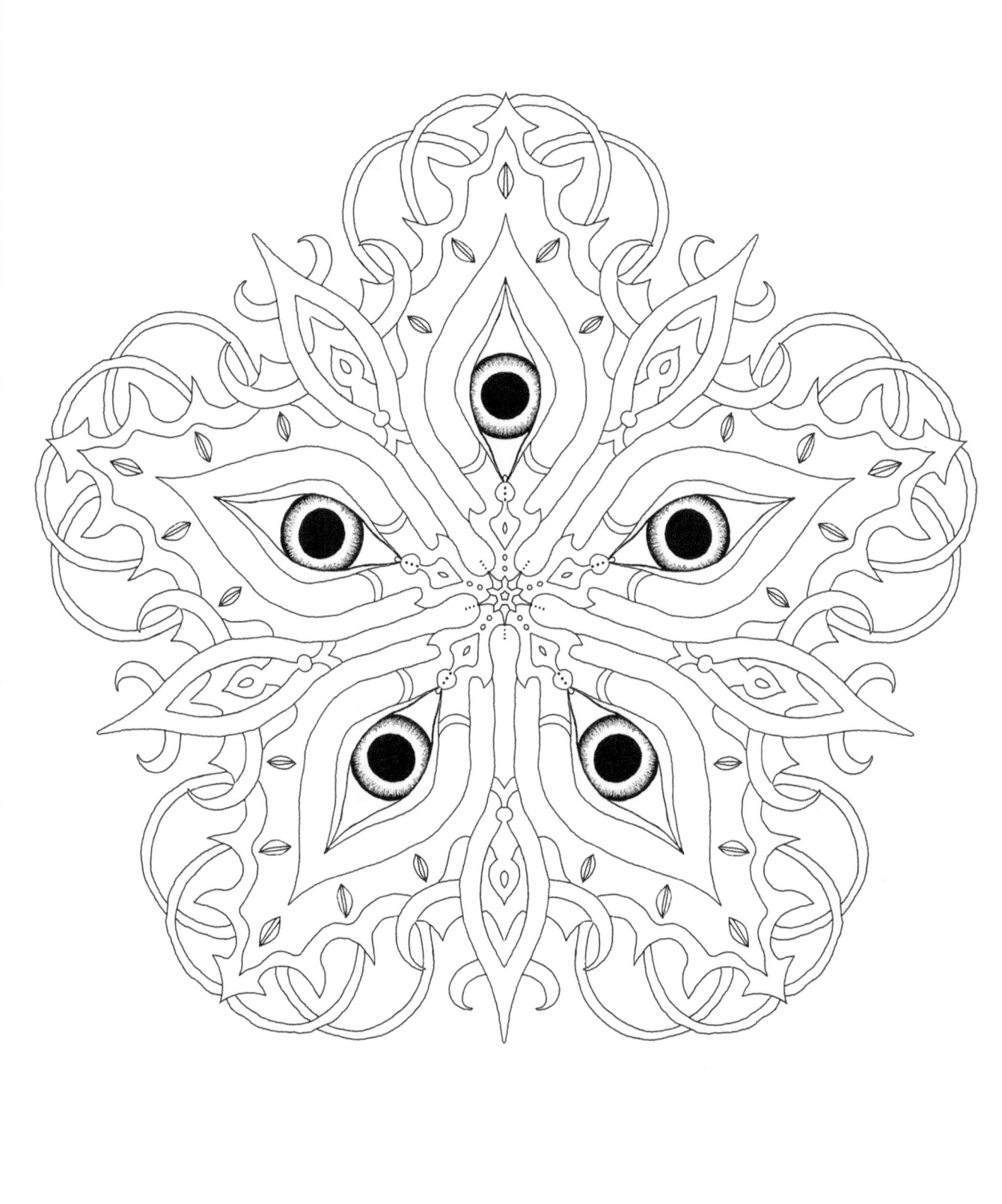

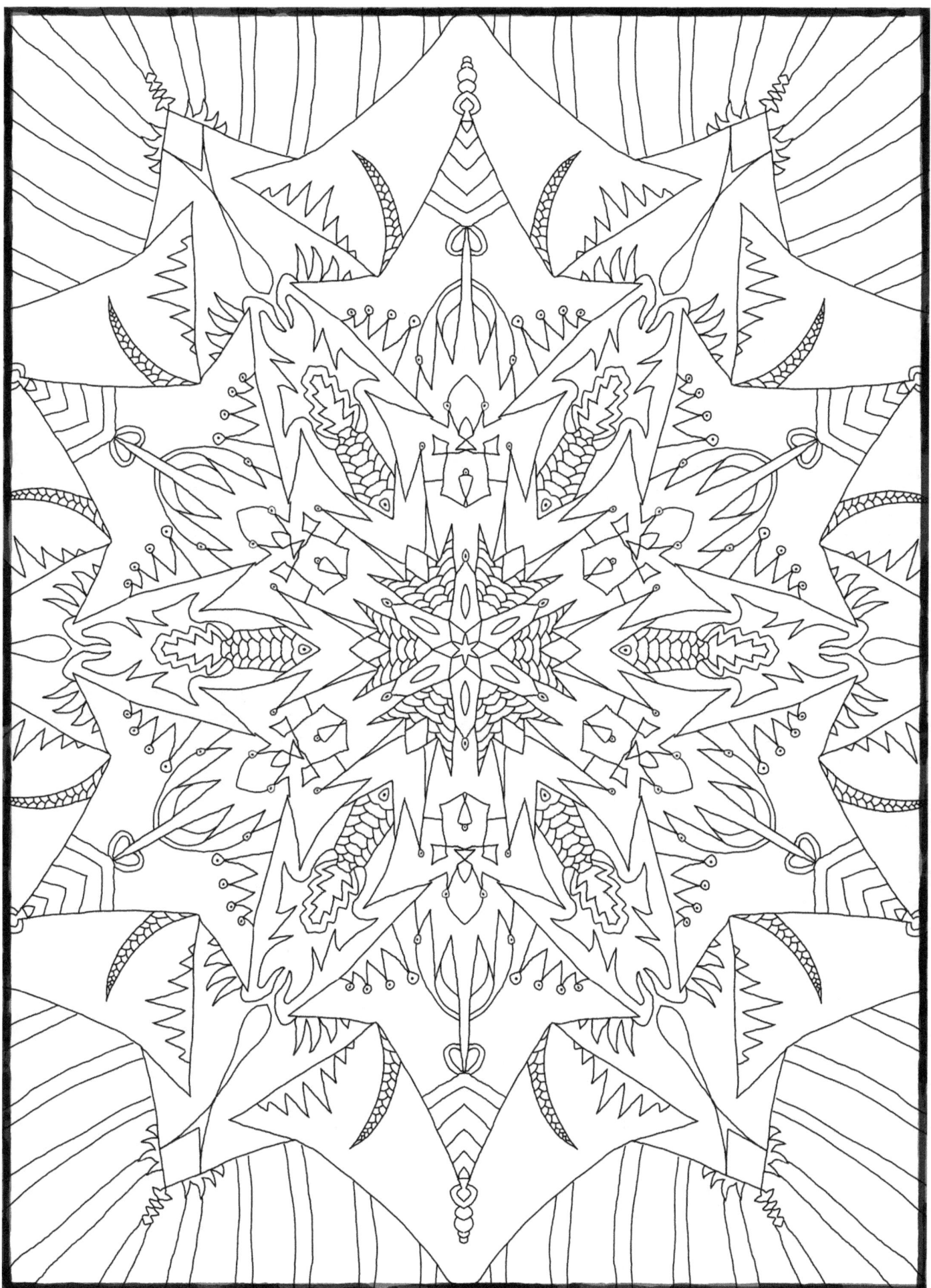

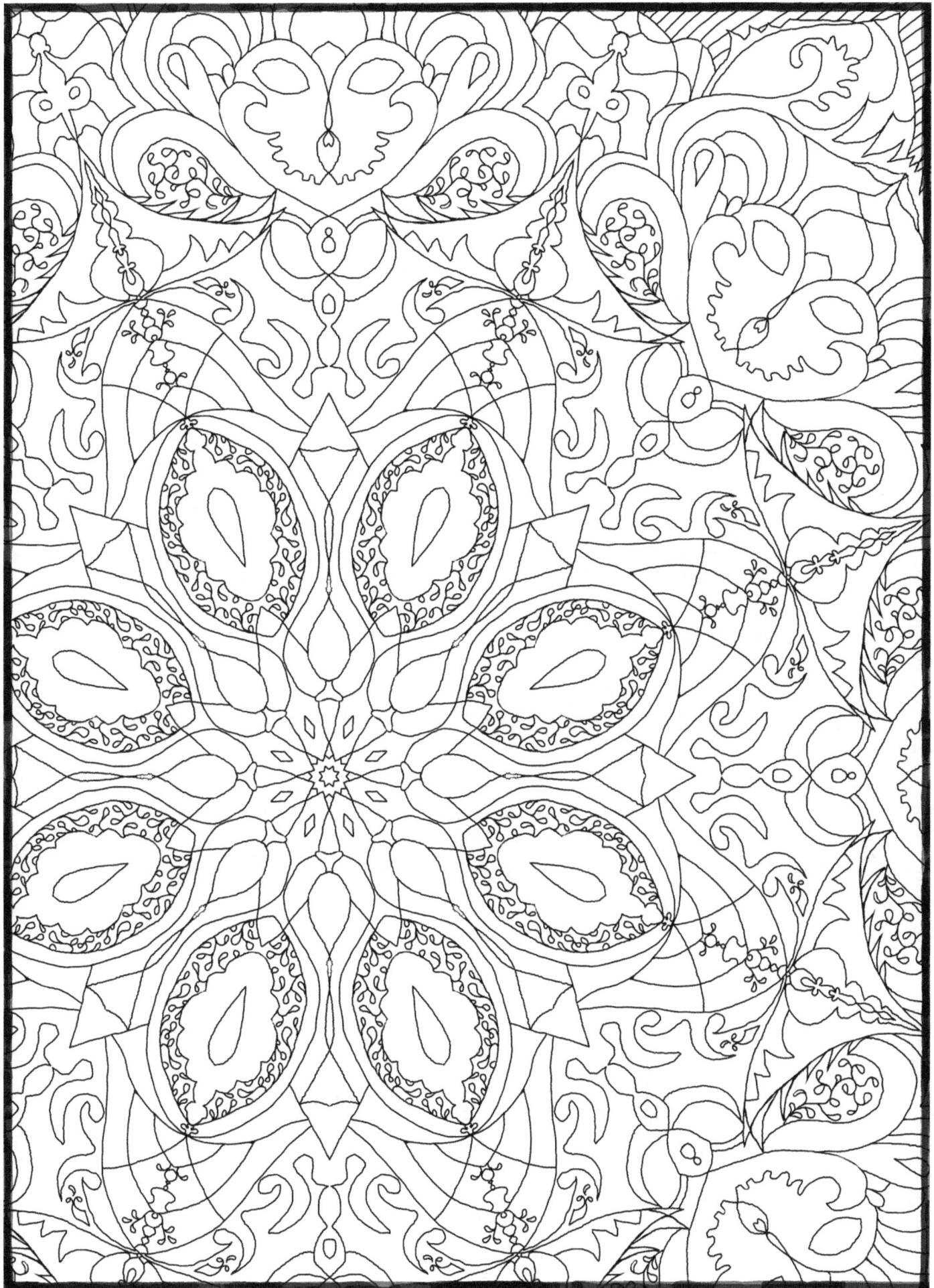

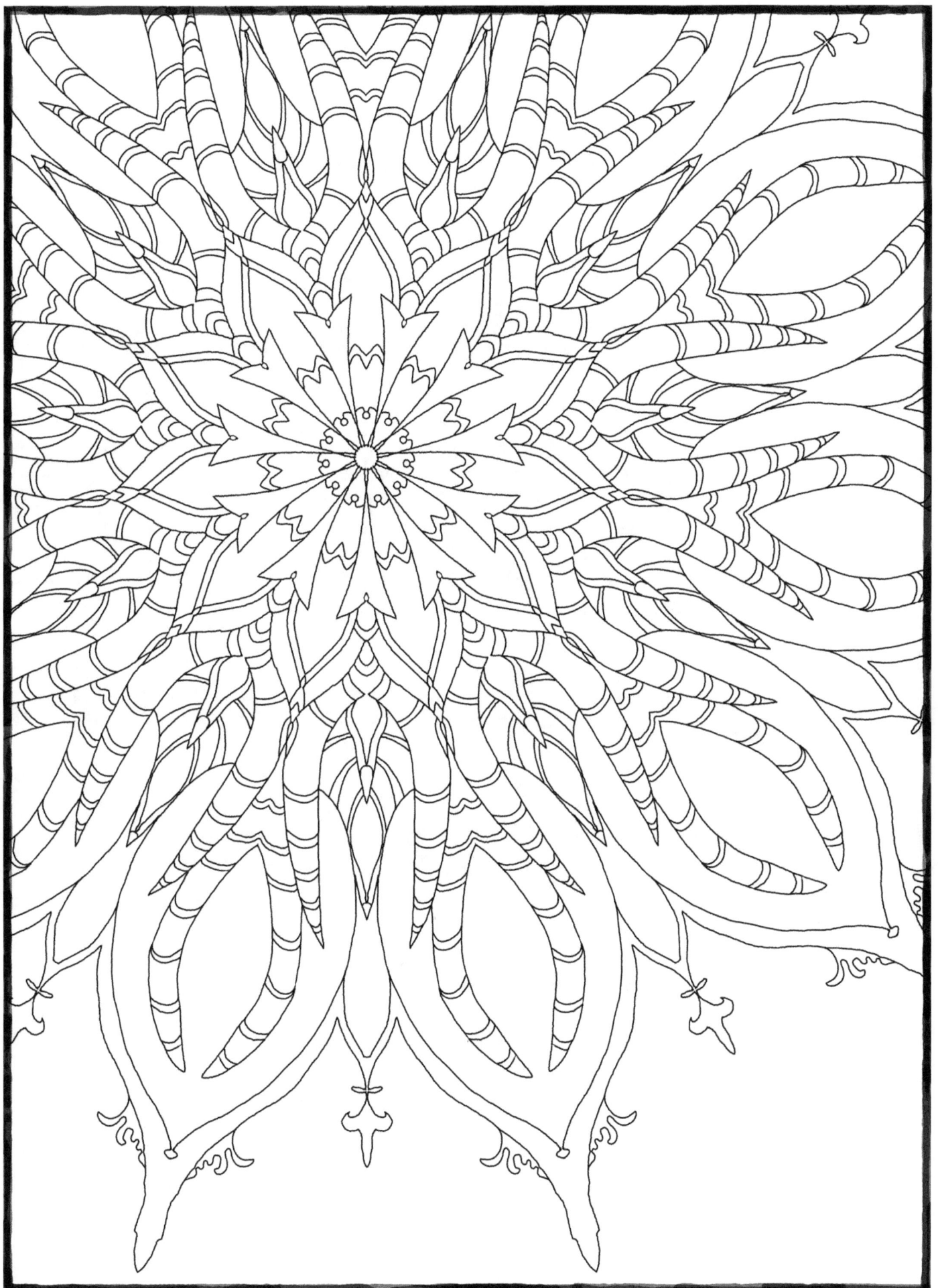

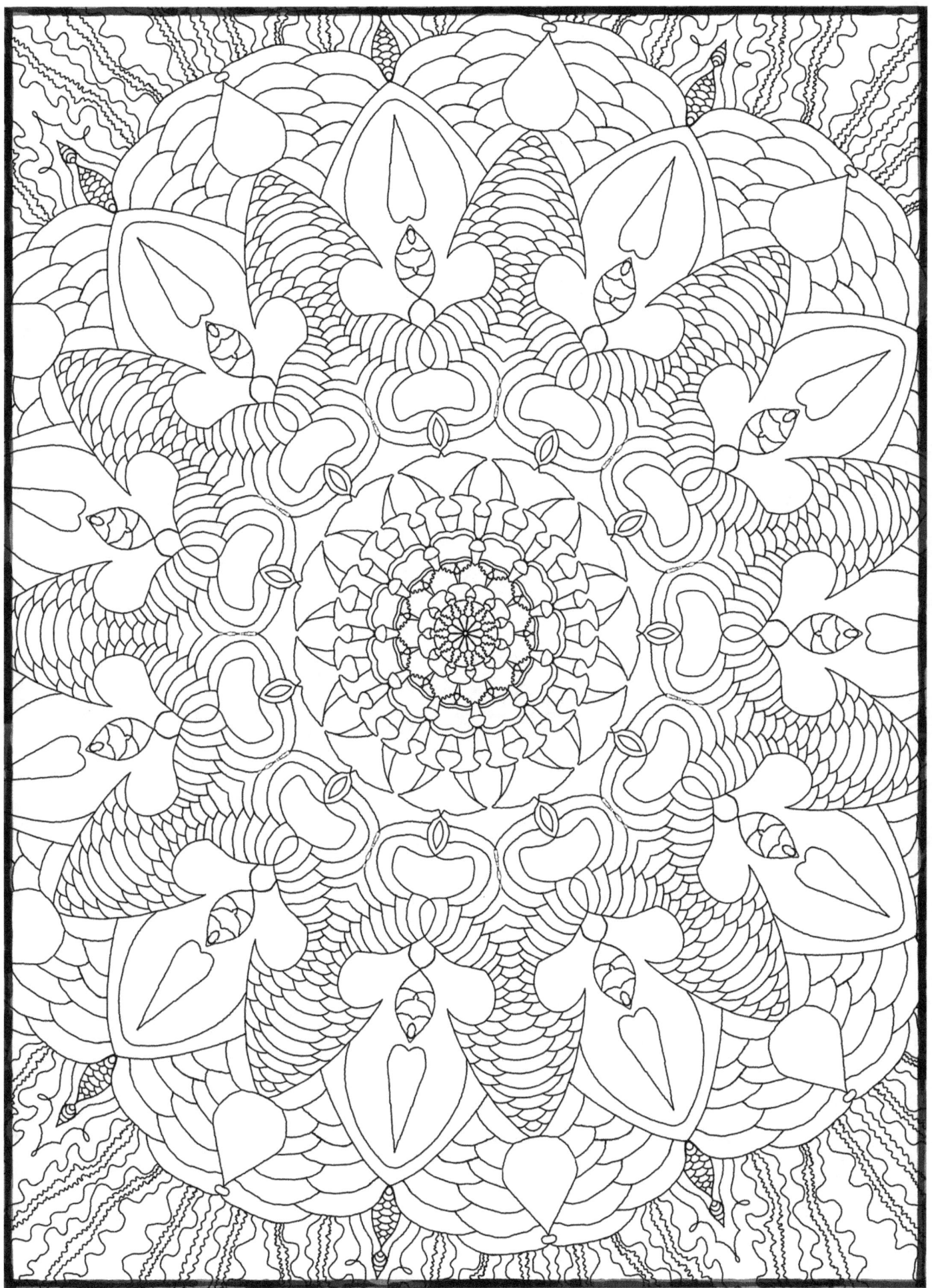

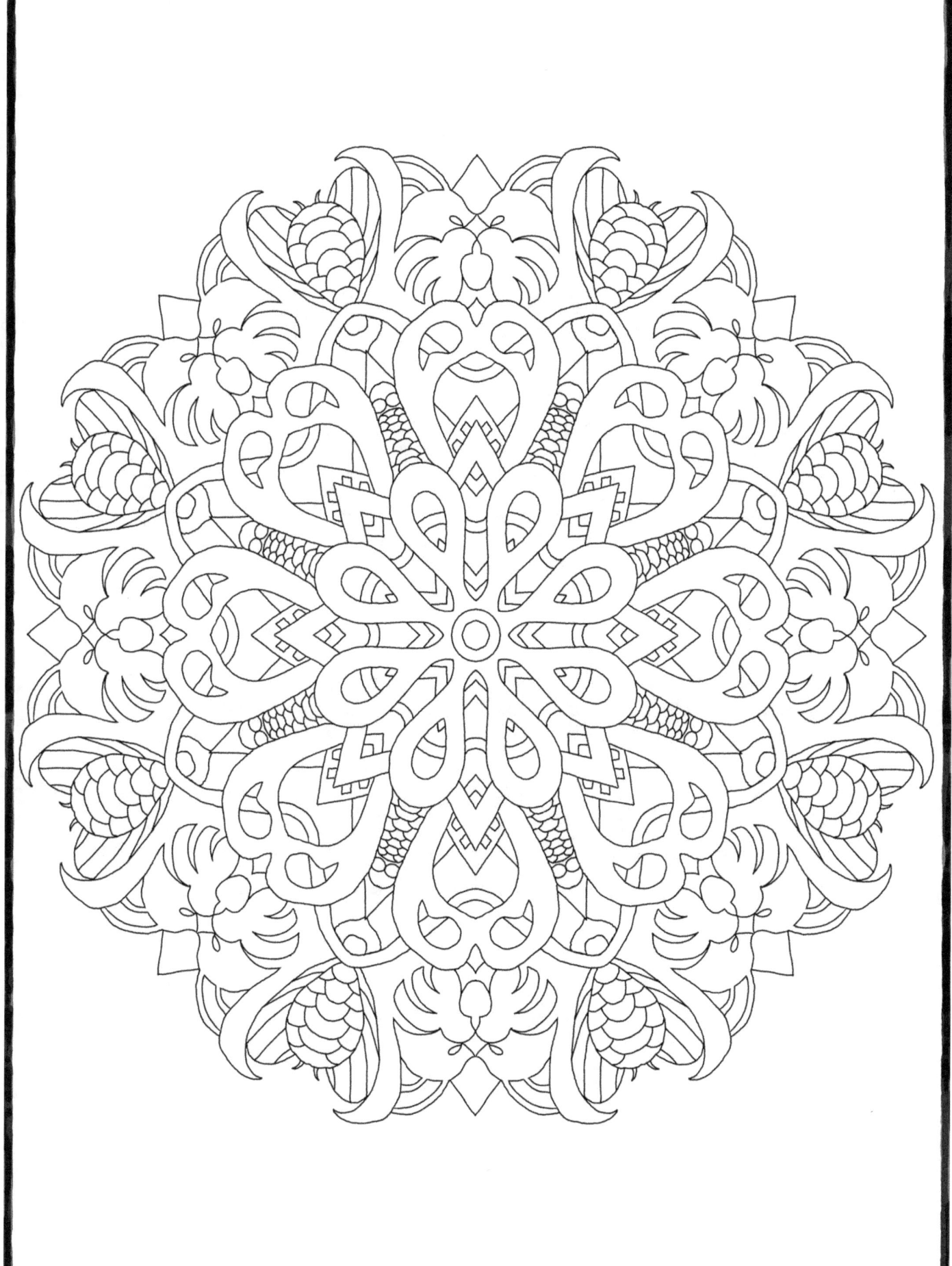

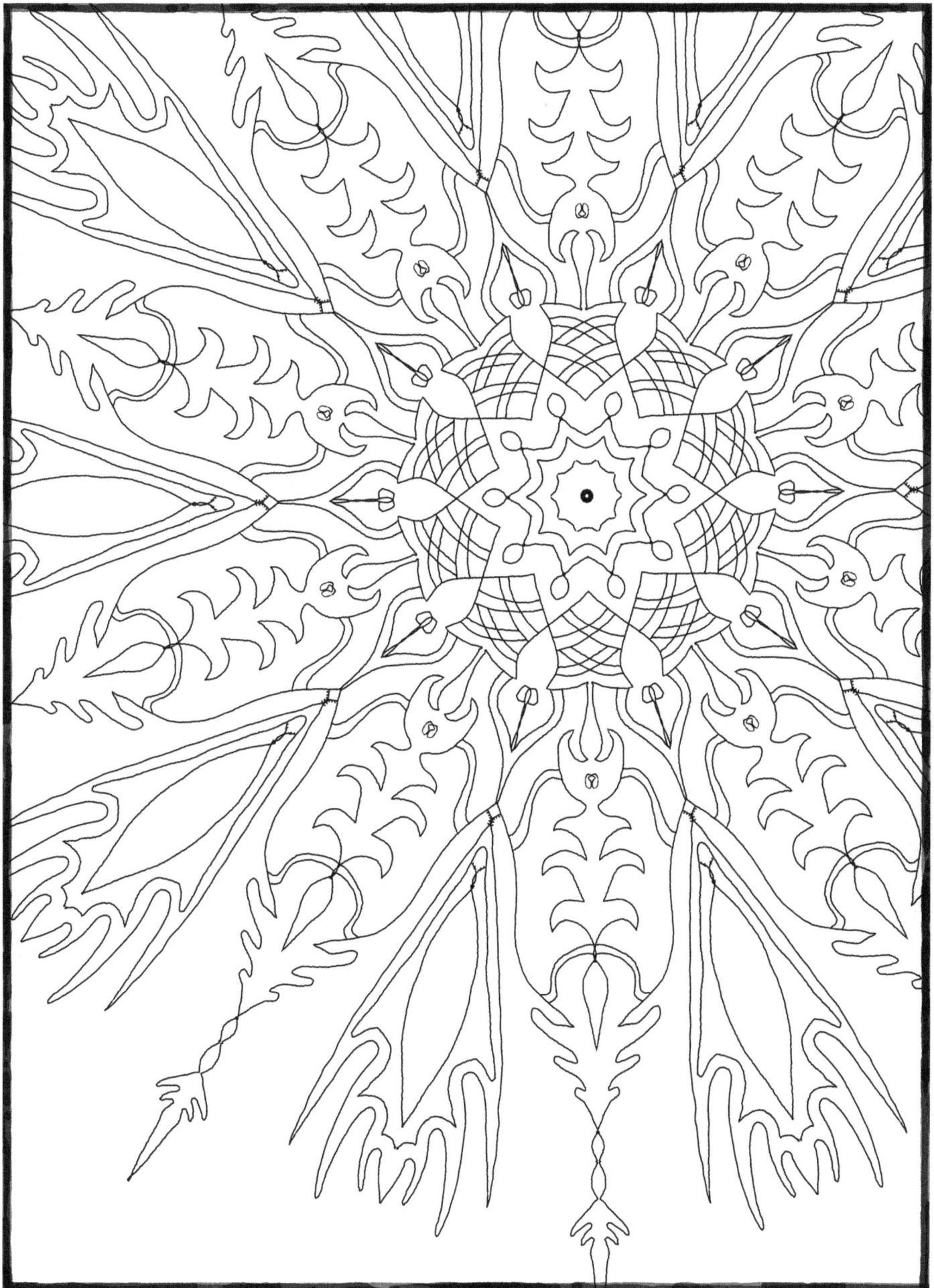

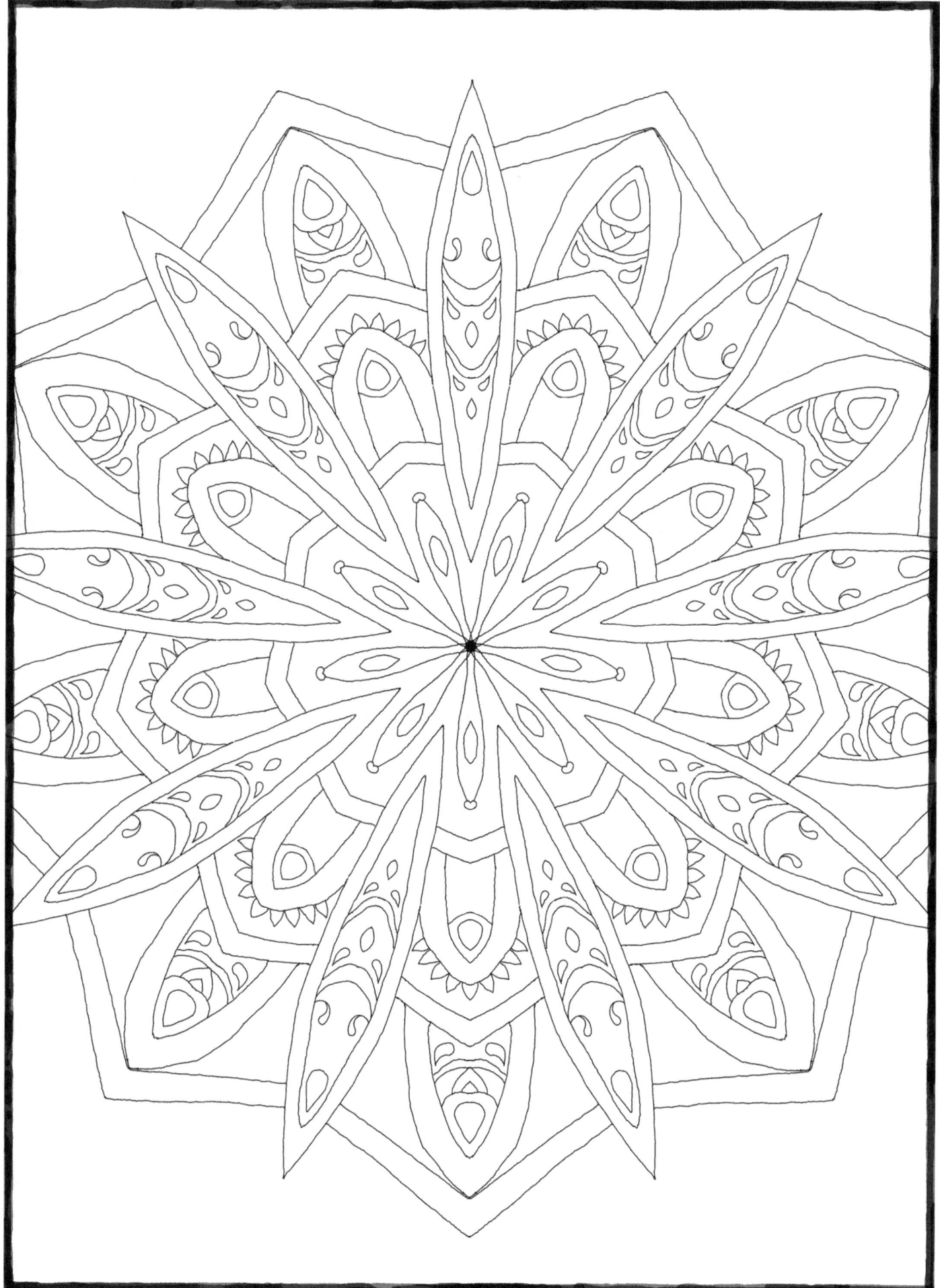

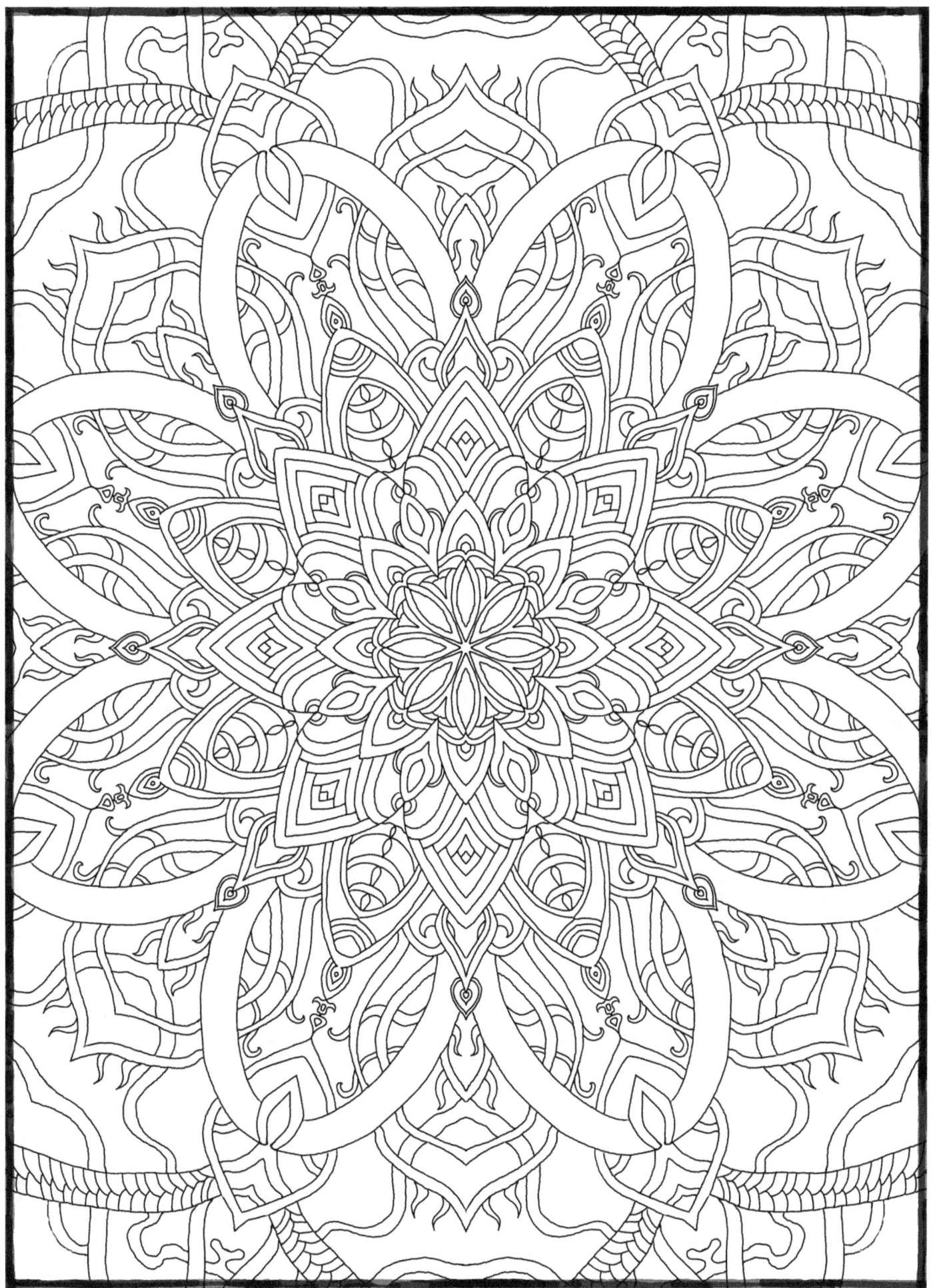

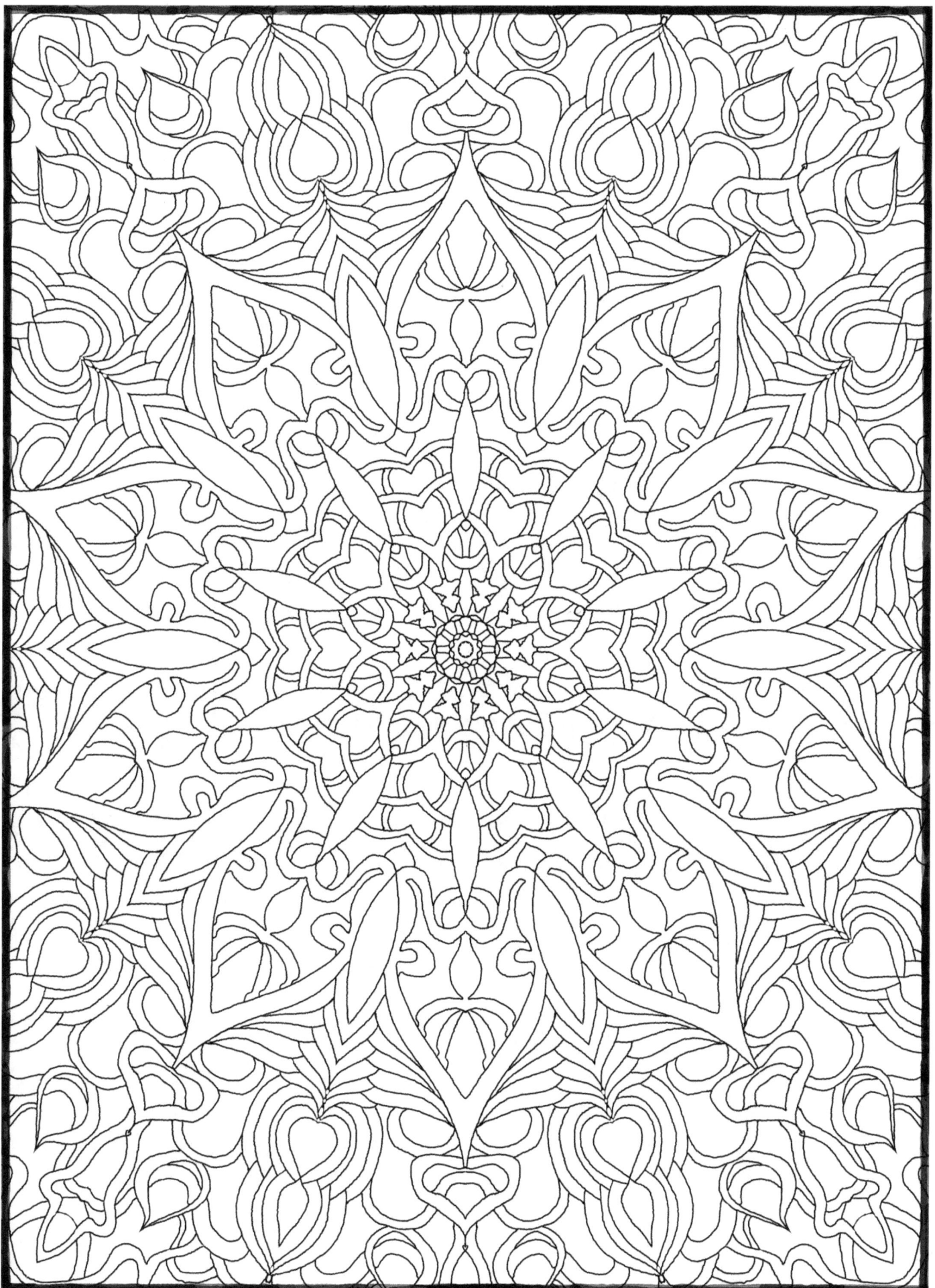

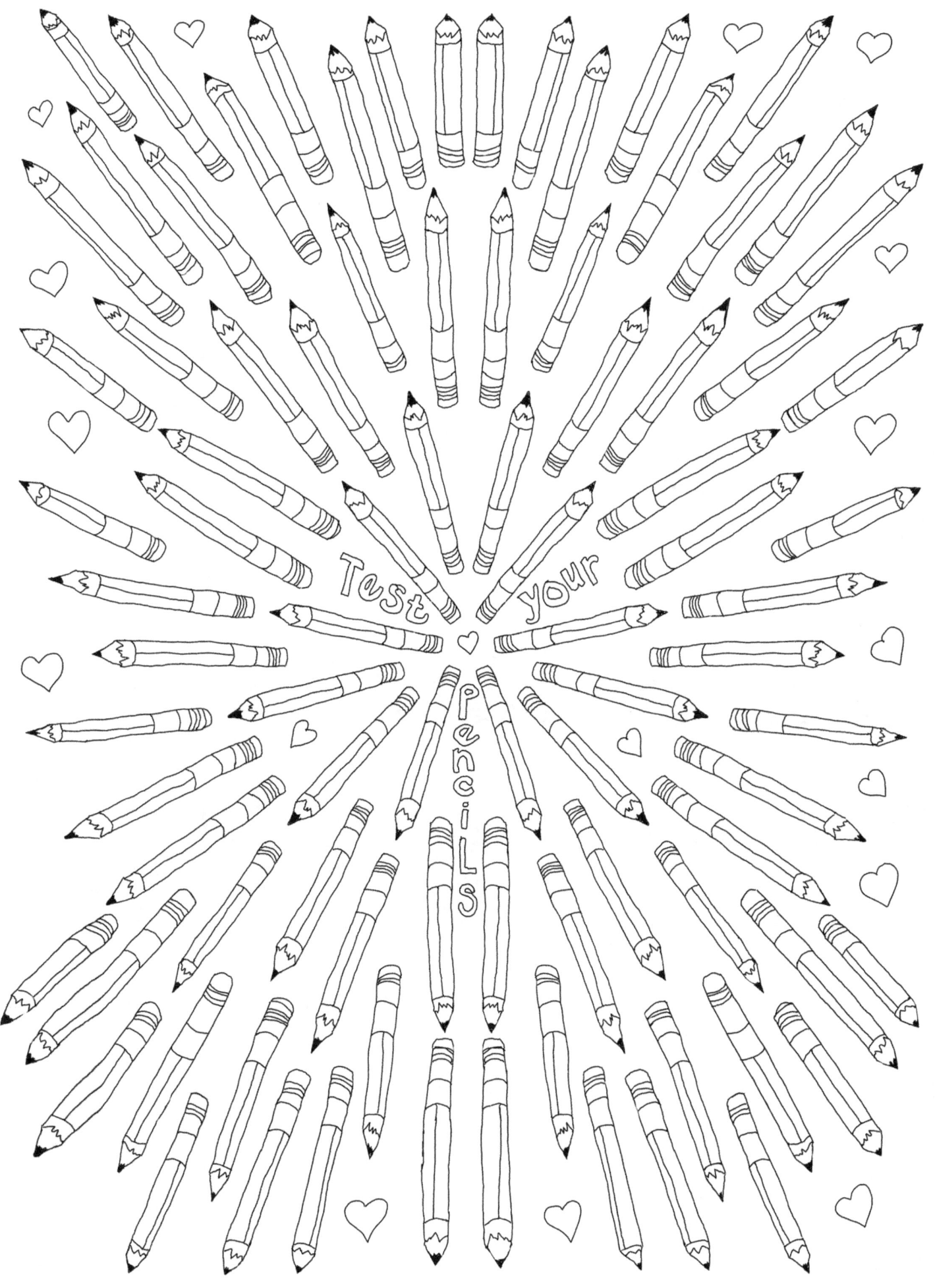

www.ingramcontent.com/pod-product-compliance
Lightning Source LLC
Chambersburg PA
CBHW080708190526
45169CB00006B/2287